Buckle Down

Buckle Down

Hartland Quay to Minehead.
One hundred and ten miles, two feet, one path.

Richard Meston

Copyright © 2023 by Richard Meston

Cover image copyright © 2023 by Harry Meston

All rights reserved. No part of this book may be reproduced or used in any manner without the written permission of the copyright owner except for the use of short quotations in a book review.

First paperback edition February 2023

(Amazon) ISBN: 979-8-3762-4486-9

Independently published

Also by Richard Meston

Other books in the South West Coast Path Series:

Half the Path
Minehead to Penzance in 9 days. Via the pub.

Buckle Up
The five-year journey to the end of a 100-mile foot race.

Flippin' Hell!
The seed was sown 14 years ago… now it's time to run 84 miles across 185 million years of coast line.

For Sophie.

*Mad and maddening,
tough and sensitive,
kind and caring,
you're a very, very special human.*

And you're definitely one of my favourite children.

Contents

Preface xii

Acknowledgements xv

Prologue xvii

Introduction 1

1 7

2 21

3 32

4 39

5 49

6 58

7 70

8 81

9 91

10 100

11 109

12 120

13 132

14 143

15 152

16	162
17	175
18	187
19	201
20	208
21	220
22	234
23	239
24	248
25	259
26	268
27	278
Epilogue	284

Preface

I'm sat on a sofa in January 2023, laptop on – of all places – my lap, and Shaun of the Dead playing on the TV in the background. The rest of this book is written, I just have to write something amazing here to trap you into thinking the rest is worth reading. Where to start…?

Things haven't been super-duper for me over the last few months, as you'll find out if you enjoy (or endure) this book all the way to the end. But they're looking up now, and I think (…hope) I might be on my way to having sorted out a few fundamental issues that seem to plague me in the gaps between races.

The North Coast 110 was one hell of a race and spending quite bit of time over the last 3 months writing about it, then re-reading and editing the words has kept it fresh in my mind. The excitement, the fun, the tiredness, the misery, and the elation all blend together to make it one of those unforgettable experiences that at least 90% of me wants to do again. My first event with Climb South West, they've now become another in my list of purveyors of mighty fine, challenging, well organised and enjoyable (in hindsight) ultrarunning experiences.

I hope I've managed to capture some of the feeling of the race within these pages and give you a sense of what the course is like, and how you might feel as you make your way along one hundred and ten tough miles of Devon and Somerset coastal path.

I wrote my first book after wandering 220 miles of the South West Coast Path with a pack on back and bugger all experience of wild camping. The whole process of writing was incredibly cathartic, so much so that it's become a habit, a necessary therapy for me to help process the big adventures in my life - a chance to revisit and enjoy, again and again.

The first book, *Half the Path,* has me trundling from Minehead to Penzance during which I cover about 90% of the North Coast 110 course, but in the other direction, walking rather than running and taking a few days to do it.

The next two books are about ultramarathons on the coast path. *Buckle Up* covers my multi-year attempt to get to the end of the Arc of Attrition, a 100-mile foot race from Coverack in south Cornwall via Land's End to Porthtowan in north Cornwall. And *Flippin' Hell* looks at the Oner, starting at my local end of the coast path in Poole and heading a little over 80 miles across some pretty tough terrain to just around Charmouth.

Within these 4 books I cover about 350 miles of the coast path through both running ultramarathons and multi-day walking with great intentions and no real experience. I guess that means there'll be a few more books coming, as it would be a shame to stop now, wouldn't it?

A note about units.

I'm an engineer by trade, so I tend to use SI units most of the time as they're unambiguous and precise. But they don't always work very well in a novel or general conversation, so I've done something that would have had my university lecturers throwing me out of the class – I've taken some liberties with imperial and metric units for distance and height.

There is some logic to it, though. For long distances, I've gone for miles, as that's how I tend to think about running a long way. For short distances, less than about a quarter of a mile (400m), I'll go with metres – everyone knows how long a 100m straight on a running track is, right?

I've mostly gone with feet for elevation – bigger numbers are more exciting, and 1,000ft sounds better than 304.8 metres.

I just felt I should explain the initially seemingly random metres/feet/miles spread around!

There we go, all done.

Acknowledgements

The waffle lives inside my brain, but without a good number of people it would never end up on paper (so you've got these people to blame…!)

First off, thank you to my ever-suffering family. Apologies for being that bloke who sits on the far end of the sofa with a laptop and pair of noise-cancelling headphones, tapping away and generally ignoring you all!

Pat Robbins – cheers for the chat, advice and running over the Purbecks. And for the inspiration from doing even sillier things like Tor des Géants!

Rodrigo Freeman-Lopez – thanks for the various chats we had on the phone and online about the race, books to read and more.

And thanks to Bea Griffiths for the chatter and support throughout the race, and Justin and the Climb South West team for putting on a great event.

Lastly, I promised I'd acknowledge everyone who helped when I was trying to decide on the book title, so cheers to David Miller, Rodrigo Freeman, Dave Price, Giacomo Squintani,

Howard Lucas, Carl Appleby, Jim Dally, David Streeter, Richard Landsdowne-Trist and Stuart Webster!

Prologue

Ultramarathons that go through the night are a stupid idea, aren't they? I mean, it's difficult enough running a lot of miles, but add in sleep deprivation – which I don't do well – and it's just daft.

No. I'm done with ultras. Last year, I walked a lot of miles on the coast path, and that was far more civilised, far more enjoyable. I could keep the walking up all day, then get some kip at night and start over again. I think, from now on, I'm going to dump the whole through-the-night idea, and go with daytime strolls, taking in the views and enjoying the scenery. This sort of event – doing silly distances all in one go for hours and hours – is just a stupid idea!

Bea and I were part running, mostly walking as we descended off the summit and down the 600ft drop into the valley. The path was a mix of dirt track and gravelly zigzag as we approached the base of the valley, and then the ascent started on the other side. All the while, the thought of stopping cementing itself in my mind.

As we started to climb up, I opened my mouth.

"I… ", I stuttered. I couldn't quite believe I was going to say it out loud, somehow it felt like it would seal my intention. "I think I'm going to stop at the next checkpoint."

INTRODUCTION

Getting out the hole

There was no getting around it, I was in a rut. I'd been in this situation a few times before, with no target on the horizon, no event to train for, but it was beginning to get out of hand now.

In January I'd finally completed the 100-mile Arc of Attrition on my fourth attempt. Just over a month later, in early March I'd run a 45 mile ultra around Bristol with 6 days' notice and only been a few minutes off my personal best.

In April I'd taken part in the Oner, 82 miles of tough coast path trail running. It had been a race I'd been eyeing up for over a decade, and I went into it off the back of minimal, inconsistent training, somehow managing to get to the end.

And now, it was June.

What little running I had been doing had no structure, and I had no real motivation for it. I was drinking something approaching 70 units of alcohol a week, and I'd put on a good chunk of weight since April.

This was becoming a familiar story for me… I don't cope well without a target, and it's occurred to me more than once, especially recently, that I should probably try and address this issue rather than just keep finding new events…

In early June, I ran a marathon – my first in 6 years. I know that somewhat contradicts what I said above about having no target, but a marathon… well, that's just a training run, right? It wasn't a target race, in fact I'd entered it as my sister loves the course of the Hampshire Hoppit and was running it herself, and I secretly hoped that it just might be the spark that re-ignited my motivation and got me running "properly" again. It went pretty well considering my training; I guess there was still some residual fitness from having done 3 ultras in the first 4 months of the year.

I was sat at work on the Monday morning following the marathon feeling a little knackered, browsing around on Facebook when I should have been working. As I was scrolling through the countless adverts and odd posts about someone's car, a bunch of photos caught my eye. They were of various parts of the Jurassic Coast – Lulworth Cove and Durdle Door, my home ground. I figured they were just late photos from the Oner Facebook group, but on closer inspection, I found they were from some group called Climb South West, who I'd never heard of before.

Reading the post above the photos, it was from a Jurassic Coast event of various distances all the way up to one hundred and twenty miles. That's an insane distance! Obviously, being some way towards insane, I had to take a better look.

With the event having just taken place over the preceding weekend, it didn't take long to dawn on me that it would be another year or so before the Jurassic Extinction Ultra Trail event would be held again. A little despondently, I made a note to look this one up next year.

The little burst of excitement that had risen in me when I realised the photos were from a race I hadn't seen before got me thinking – who were this lot, Climb South West?

I found their website and took a good look around. There were quite a few events with results going back 4 or 5 years, so they didn't look like a "here one minute, gone the next" outfit. Founded by Justin Nicholas, the information on the site gave a sense of his enthusiasm for the outdoors – everything from mountain climbing through water sports and on to ultra-marathons There were events in Dartmoor, and Wales, and Exmoor… hmmm… what's this one… the North Coast 110?

One hundred and ten miles from Hartland Quay to Minehead.

I liked the look of that. I liked it a lot!

It was long, which was a good start, a real challenge. And it was set on a stretch of the coast path that I mostly knew, or at least had been on once. Last year, I'd attempted to walk from Minehead to Poole, the full 630 miles of the South West Coast Path. It hadn't gone to plan, but I had covered over 90% of the route of this race, only going in the other direction. It was a bit of coastline that I was particularly fond of - it would be fantastic to revisit it.

Today was June 13th, and the race was on October 7th, just over 16 weeks away. That's a perfect chunk of time for training. I downloaded the event information pack and read through the details. Mandatory kit was all as expected, I met all the entry requirements, the cut-offs looked achievable.

I think I'd just found my next event.

When I got home after work on that Monday, I had a chat with my wife, Eva. She was delighted that I'd found some another event – she loves it when I'm out running all the time, then disappear off for a few days, then come back knackered, talking incessantly about some bloody race! But she also understands that I'm a bit of an oddball, and that I'd been a bit lost with no event to target, so was happy – well, tolerant – of me doing it.

I'd only found the race that day, I didn't want to make a big decision – one that would involve a lot of training and spending a fair chunk of money – without having at least a bit of thinking about it. I said to Eva that I'd sleep on it and see how I felt tomorrow, but in reality, my head had already made the decision.

There was another reason I was waiting until the Tuesday as well, a slightly odd sentimental one.

And now it was here. The 14th of June was my Mum's birthday, and she had died a few years ago on October 8th – the same day as the North Coast 110 race finished. It seemed like a sign – a contrived one, but a couple of little hooks that I could use to justify entering.

When looking at some details about the race, I remembered a friend I knew on Facebook – Rodrigo Freeman – had run it the previous year, so I sent him a message to see what he thought of it and if he had any advice.

When the response comes back as "Yep, the NC110 is a great race, I recommend", and "The guys at Climb South West are great," there was no going back now.

A smidge under £200 later, I had my entry and transport to the start booked for the North Coast 110. Time to get training!

Having got into the habit of writing books about long races recently, I thought that this time I'd write some notes down *before* the event. Here were the points I wrote down about how I was feeling, having just entered:

1. It scares the shit out of me. That's a good thing though, isn't it more fun doing something that scares you a bit?
2. It's 10 miles more than the Arc, which took me 4 years to complete. I don't really want to end up spending the next 4 years trying to finish this race too! But on the plus side, having already covered over 90% of the race route on my walk last year, I know the terrain is generally far less technical than the Arc.
3. My walk last year had a few gaps between Minehead and Penzance, but I had covered the route of the race as far as a little past Clovelly. It would be great to fill in that missing 10 miles or so between Clovelly and Hartland Quay, but also to revisit all the other places again.
4. I'm genuinely, ridiculously excited! I have a plan, a target and I'm already imagining myself heading into the night, the excitement of the adventure clear in my mind.
5. I'd never done an event with Climb South West. It will be interesting to see what they are like, and hopefully it will open up another avenue of decent adventures to look at in future.
6. There's a big distance between the aid stations – more than 20 miles between several of them. With only 20 or 30 people in the race (judging by results from previous years), I need to be truly self-sufficient for those big sections, hopefully giving it the feel of the first Arc race

I did back in 2018, when there was much less support on the course.

All positive and exciting, time to get on with preparing myself to run 110 miles!

1

Training

June 2022

I entered the race on a Tuesday. On the Friday of that week, it was 16 weeks until race day. Time for a plan, so I jotted down a few ideas, a bunch of pretty standard and obvious stuff that I'd used before for races.

First off, I'd get back to a low-carb diet. I find this type of diet to work really well for me for ultradistance events, where I'm going slowly for a long time. With sixteen weeks to adapt, I was hoping that by race day I'd be needing half the amount of carbohydrates than I would have had I been eating a standard diet. The other benefit is that I tend to lose weight quickly and reliably when I cut carbohydrates, and I could really do with losing the good chunk I'd recently put on before race day.

The other thing that had to go was alcohol. I needed to seriously cut down, and now I had a target and some motivation, it should be... easy? Yeah, maybe not *easy*, but hopefully doable.

A phone call with Rodrigo gave me some great tips and information about the race, including one of his training tools. He told me about running for 10 consecutive days of 10-15 miles each day, the idea being to keep the effort so low that you relatively easily manage the day-after-day approach. An interesting thought, and one I added to my mental list of training ideas.

One thing I had learnt while doing some relatively serious and focussed marathon training a few years back was that I don't have a long attention span when it comes to training plans. I can manage 8 weeks at a push, but any longer and I go off the boil, finding excuses and not sticking to what I should be doing. That ends up with me feeling like it's all going down the pan, and I end up backing right off before the event.

With that in mind, I'd split this 16-week block into 4 weeks of "base building", no firm structure, just concentrating on getting comfortable at slow runs up to about 10 miles, losing a bit of weight and getting myself ready to work a bit harder. I'd aim to get my running up to somewhere between 40 and 50 miles per week and try to add in 10-20 miles of fast walking too.

The middle 8 weeks would be the focused section. I hadn't decided on details, but I'd put in lots of hills and longer runs, the sort of stuff that builds both physical and mental resilience.

The last 4 weeks… that would just be an attempt to keep the fitness without getting bored. And also, a bit of a buffer zone, should I miss a week or two for some reason during the 8 weeks of harder effort.

I was enthusiastic to start, as is always the way. I cut the carbs right down, along with the alcohol, and ran 3 days in a row which was something I hadn't done for a while. I felt tired and lethargic and wasn't sleeping well, but I put this down to the change in my diet, and also the fact that work had been particularly busy recently. I kind-of forgot that I had run a marathon the previous weekend as well, something which I don't think I really allowed myself full time to recover from. After all, it was only a marathon, right?

I accidentally found myself out with a friend on that first Saturday, and 6 beers and a kebab later, I was back home thinking that, as it was Father's Day the following day, I might as well have that as a day off. I had a few more beers that day too, after all, I had been good *most* of the previous week – and I had just run a marathon – so it was easy to justify a "treat". Can you spot where I go wrong?

The weeks went on in a similar fashion. I kept my "Moanday" group appointment, a faster social run generally averaging a little quicker than 8-minute miles for 9 or 10 miles as my one and only fast run of the week. I was struggling to hit 40 miles each week, but I was getting in about 15 miles of fast walking. Despite the lapses in my eating and drinking, I was beginning to see improvements – getting a little fitter, a little faster, a little better at running. The fact this was happening even with all that crap eating and drinking wasn't helping with me to convince myself to be healthier.

We had a week family holiday in Switzerland booked for the end of July in Saas-Fee, an area we'd been to a couple of times before. It's a popular winter ski resort, but all our visits have been in summer, and I knew just how great the alpine hills around there were for running. I hadn't done many hills in my training so far, but I wanted to be able to make the most of the hills on the holiday, so I joined the local gym on a great deal – £30 for a bit over 2 months membership! – so I could use the treadmill to simulate walking up hills. With the treadmill on 15%, each mile takes you up the equivalent of 792ft, and while not technically identical to climbing a real hill, it was the best I could do locally. Previous experience had shown me that this treadmill slogging in the gym did make a significant different to my climbing ability.

It was hard work on the first day, I managed 2 miles, so just over 1,500ft ascent. But a few weeks later, just before we headed off to Switzerland, I'd managed to total the best part of 20,000ft of treadmill climbing. My legs still ached when doing it, but I was getting stronger and faster on the climbs, and I hoped it would mean I could make the most of those Swiss hills.

We arrived in Saas-Fee on a Wednesday afternoon. The town is 6,000ft (1,800m) above sea level, so it's not unusual to feel a little out of breath for the first few days. We only had a week there, though, so I didn't want to wait too long before running.

On the second day, I headed up to a little place called Hannig and then straight back down, a 1,800ft climb and descent in a little under 5 miles. It was pouring with rain – a first for me in Switzerland – and sections of the slatey trail and grassy ground were lethally slippery in places, so I was taking it pretty cautiously. I still managed to beat my best time from my last run in Saas-Fee some 8 years previously by almost 20 minutes!

That's quite a boost. I wasn't feeling particularly fit and was in the early stages of trying to train my way out of an over-eating, over-drinking rut, but it looked like the accumulation of all the training I'd done over those 8 years had definitely had some effect on my general ability to run up and down hills.

Fifteen hours after the first run, my legs objected somewhat to another one, but I dragged them up 2,500 ft to Mallig, then back down half way to meet the rest of my family, who'd sensibly come up by cable car for breakfast in the café.

Sunday saw me head up to Plattjen, somewhere I'd not been before on foot. The cable car was out of action for the summer season, so it was just me on my own going up and down there. The terrain was a little more technical, rocky and winding, and the August sun was out in full force making it a hot climb. Being the third run with a decent amount of elevation in 3 days, I was definitely feeling the effort, but that was good – proof my aching legs could still climb and descend even if they didn't feel the best they could. All useful mental and physical training for when you're 24 hours into an ultramarathon, feeling exhausted and still have 30 or 40 miles left to go.

I had a day off running, then on our last full day I went up to Längfluh, a plateau just over 3,300ft (1,000m) above the town. I started at the bottom, the rest of my family went via cable car to Spielboden about two-thirds of the way up. Inspired by my silly running around in the mountains, my oldest son, Harry, walked from there to the top while the others got the cable car the rest of the way.

As I came through Spielboden, I knew Harry was somewhere ahead of me, which made this a race! I really tried to push on the final section to catch him up, working hard and enjoying the feeling, knowing that it was my last big climb and tomorrow we'd be going home. I just caught sight of him at the very end, with him beating me to the top by less than a minute!

We all sat around and had a coffee, then walked around admiring the views from this great height. When it was time to go, I ran back down, trying to race the other lot in their cable car. I took a new route down that I hadn't used before, with lots of switchbacks on a rocky trail that really taxed my ankles, twisting them a few times – I was very grateful for the support from my poles at times down there.

Running was hard work mentally when I got back from Switzerland. The dark grey streets of urban Dorset aren't quite as inspiring as the fantastic ascents and descents of the Alps, with beautiful snow-capped mountain views everywhere you look. I got back to the treadmill at the gym, and planned some runs in the local Purbeck hills, the nearest place which offered some descent elevation change in a relatively short distance.

I seemed to be trying to cut down on alcohol and eat better on a weekly basis – a few days of doing it right gave me all the ammo I needed to justify the rest of the week doing it all wrong. The same thing happened with press-ups, squats, and yoga, a few days on, a few days off – it was all very sporadic.

A good friend who I run with most weeks, Pat Robbins, was doing a lot of hill training for his upcoming race, the considerably more challenging Tor des Géants, a 330km non-stop mountain race with around 80,000ft (yes, you read that right) of climbing! We ran together in the Purbecks on one occasion, doing reps up and down the biggest hills we could find. I wasn't too terrible at this point, having had all the treadmill sessions and the week in the Alps in my legs, but it was inspiring to see someone who could *really* run the hills doing a good few reps more than me over the same time!

With 6 weeks to go, I thought I'd give Rodrigo's ten-day plan a shot. It happened by accident really, in that I did a couple of unplanned 10 mile runs on consecutive days and figured I'd started now, I might as well carry on.

Ten miles is both quite a long way, and not all that far. The first couple of days were easy, the next couple were mentally quite hard, and then I got into a routine and was actually quite disappointed to stop at the end of day 10, although it did give me an hour-and-a-half back each day. I kept the effort low for most of the runs, and it was a good feeling to know that 10 miles can just get done without a huge amount of thought.

After those 10 days, I was back treadmill climbing and at the peak I managed to cover 4 miles with a climb of just under 3,200ft in a little under 50 minutes, the fastest I'd ever completed it.

Things were actually starting to look pretty good – I was better at climbing hills than I'd probably ever been in my life and was finding I could cover 10 miles day after day without any issues. The only thing missing really was a test of running for a long time – my longest run during this training block had been about 16 miles. I did hope, though, that previous experience would help me keep going the distance as long as I had the general fitness in the first place.

In the last month before the race, I managed two medium-long runs of around 16 miles, and some more sessions out in the Purbeck hills where I witnessed a couple of amazing sunsets around Lulworth Cove and Durdle Door. It's moments like that which make me genuinely grateful for being able to be out and about, running up and down hills with such stunning displays of nature on show.

I carried on bouncing around with drinking and eating, but as race day approached, I was in about the right ballpark – the majority of my eating relatively healthy, and the majority of my drinking relatively non-alcoholic.

Two weeks out from race day I cut out all caffeine, something I do for all long ultras, so those overnight coffees during the race would work their magic when I really needed them.

The only real issue was that work had gone absolutely mad over the last month or two, and I felt like I didn't have a minute to spare outside of working and training. Combined with the increased training load, my sleep was back to being disrupted and I wasn't really feeling very recovered at any point, even after my days off, which was a bit of a concern.

With a week to go, I was happy with having finally eaten fairly well and not drunk too much in the preceding week. Work had continued to be mentally draining, and at the end of the work week I tried to unwind with one final splurge before my 7-day pre-race route kicked in, downing 4 beers and most of the cupboard full of chocolate. Bloody idiot!

On the Saturday before race day, I started my routine of 5 days of very low carbs and ran a surprisingly easy 16 miler in the afternoon. The last run on the Monday was really good too, a great psychological boost, especially after that long run just 2 days before. There was to be no more running now, I was going to hold on to that good feeling of being vaguely fit and prepared.

In the past, in the weeks approaching a race – especially a new one – I would spend literally hours poring over maps, instructions and previous race reports, create spreadsheets with pace calculations and more. But at the office, the work I was doing was both enjoyable and important, so I hadn't found the time to do any real preparation for the race.

During the final week, just a day or two before the race, I spent a little time looking at things like sunrise and sunset times so I could roughly work out where it would get dark, allowing me to plan what to put in drop bags. I created a list on my phone, and kept adding things as I remembered, hoping that when it came to packing the list would have everything I needed.

There was also the matter of filling up my watch and handheld GPS with route files so that I had a helping hand to guide me in the right direction, otherwise, with my sense of direction, I'd end up in St Ives. Or Cardiff.

I took the official race GPX file from the website, which was quite coarse with relatively few points, and overlaid my walk the previous year, so that I had both more detail and more accurate distance calculations when the tracks were loaded onto my watch. Although I checked over the whole route to make sure my detailed track matched the official route, it takes quite a while to check through 110 miles and I wasn't paying quite as much attention as I should have, something which I've since learnt is worth spending the extra few minutes on!

I also spent a little while calculating some times for various points along the route. I used Rodrigo's times from the previous year as one set, and calculated the very latest that I could be at spots along the route and still get to the finish before the cutoff of 38 hours. Finally, I worked out a set that I hoped I could achieve, with a finish just before 6pm – around 34 hours in total. That would give me 4 hours to play with in case things went very wrong!

With all the numbers calculated, I printed out 3 shrunk-down copies of the timing list, "laminated" them with strips of sticky tape to protect them from rain and sweat, then stuck them in various easily accessible places in my pack.

The weather was getting colder in late September. Not by a huge amount, but 2022 was the year of the Great Energy Price Rise, where gas prices tripled and electricity prices more than doubled between April and October. Little drops in temperature were quite noticeable, mainly due to there being no chance in hell of me turning the heating on until the temperature got below zero! It did, however, make me appreciate – or rather remind me – how cold it might get during the night. I didn't want to be in the position I was back in April during the Oner, where I had warmer clothes in the pack on my back, but as they were reserved for emergencies, they were fairly inaccessible, certainly when I was so cold that I didn't want to stop moving. I made the decision this time round to ensure that I was wearing a warm layer, and a second was *easily* accessible in my pack should I need it.

Those 5 days of eating a strict low carbohydrate diet just before the race were actually surprisingly easy. Once I get close enough – within the final week – there's no time to recover if I deviate from the plan, so it becomes a no-brainer. Generally, when my brain gets involved, things go awry, so a no-brainer is the best situation for me to be in. Although I didn't run, I did quite a bit of fast walking during those 5 days too, all of which felt… fine. No real lack of energy, I felt ready.

On the Wednesday evening, I packed my race vest and drop bags with a few changes to my normal routine, based on experiences over the last few ultras. First, I usually stick a whole selection of anything first-aid related in a little zip-up kit which goes in the emergency drybag against my back. On occasions in previous events, I wanted simple things like a plaster from the pack but didn't bother as it was too awkward to get to. This time round, I adjusted the emergency pack to only contain things that I would use when the shit really hit the fan, and put a few small things I was more likely to need during a normal race – plasters, paracetamol, that sort of thing – more easily accessibly in my vest. This meant potentially duplicating some things in the back of my pack, but the weight of a few more plasters in the pack was unlikely to vastly change the outcome of my race.

I had a cold-and-wet-weather drybag stuffed in the side of my pack, easily accessible without having to take the pack off. I kept this to a minimum of useful stuff: warm gloves, waterproof over-gloves, waterproof shorts, and a hat. If my hands got cold, my head got cold, or it started raining heavily, I could sort it quickly and easily.

The main section of the pack had the usual selection of drybags, one with a main and backup headtorch, another with a spare soft flask just in case of emergency (they're very light, why not?) and my Salomon Pulse belt for carrying poles against my hips when I didn't want them in my hands. I also had a food bag with enough nutrition to last the considerable distance between the aid stations at 40 and 75 miles. Only then would I have access to my drop bag.

The last drybag was my gadget-and-everything-else bag which had inside my MP3 player, a little power bank with enough charge to shock my phone or watch back to life if it needed resuscitation, various cables for charging, those extra easily accessible paracetamol and plasters, plus £10 and a bank card in case I passed a supermarket, chip shop or pub that didn't take Apple Pay.

Food-wise, I opted for fewer flapjacks than I normally take. For the last few ultramarathons, I'd carried a bunch of them around untouched for somewhere between 80 and 100 miles, and it seemed unnecessary to repeat that another time. Instead, I filled little food bags with various nuts, seed and raisins. Although I hadn't tried it under race conditions (a bit naughty!), I could usually tolerate nuts at any point, so I was hoping the mix of fats and proteins from the nuts, along with carbs from the dried fruit, would remain palatable throughout the race. There were also a few Peperami and just one or two sweeter bars for a bit of sugar… if I could stomach them.

And that's about it. Training done. Kit sorted. All I had to do now was get to the race, then get the race done. How hard can it be?

	Miles	RFL	Calc	Limit	Cutoff
Start	0	07:30	07:30	07:30	
Clovelly	9.8	10:08	09:56	10:09	
Peppercombe	16.3	11:53	11:32	11:54	
Edge of Ho!	20.6	13:08	12:36	13:04	
Appledore	25.6	14:23	13:47	14:21	
Bideford (Bridge)	28.8	15:11	14:33	15:11	
Instow (Marines Stuff)	32.3	15:55	15:23	16:05	
Barnstaple (CP)	37.9	17:15	16:42	17:32	2100
Velator	43.2	19:15	18:17	19:15	
Croyde	51.7	21:42	20:49	22:01	
Woolacombe (Centre)	57.5	23:43	22:33	23:54	
Ilfracombe (Quay)	66.1	03:15	01:54	03:34	
Combe Martin (CP)	72.3	06:18	04:19	06:12	0800
Heddon Valley (End)	80.1	08:50	07:23	09:32	
Lynton	86.3	10:25	09:50	12:12	1300
Culbone	96.3	13:47	13:26	16:07	
Porlock Wier	98.1	14:19	14:05	16:50	1700
Bossington	102	15:35	15:22	18:14	
Selworthy Beacon (ish)	104	16:23	16:01	18:57	
End	109	18:09	17:40	20:45	2130

This was the timing chart that I had in my pack. The *Miles* and *Cutoff* columns are obvious. *RFL* is the time Rodrigo (Freeman-Lopez) hit the aid stations during his race, and *Calc* is my calculated target times. *Limit* is about the last time that I could get to each point and still complete the race in time.

2

SLOTH

Thursday, 6th October 2022

Five thirty in the morning is a pretty rubbish time to wake up. I know a lot of people do and, if I'm honest, I'd quite like to get into the habit of waking up early as I think I'd probably be more productive. But I'm not used to it, and the tuneful alarm of Eva's phone did nothing to soften the metaphorical blow.

My brain started waking, my eyes stayed firmly shut and my body flatly refused to do anything even approaching getting up. As the foggy clouds coalesced into my first thought of the day, it dawned on me… this was when it all kicked off!

I reached my arm over and turned on the bedside light, finally opening my eyes and, after being blinded by said bedside light, quickly closing them again. I lay there, with the light seeping through my eyelids, contemplating the night I'd just had.

Usually, I have a rubbish sleep on the night-before-the-night-before a race. I put it down to nervousness about the event, or rather what I call the "car parking" – everything involved in getting to the start of the event. But two nights out, I'm not normally tired enough to ensure a deep sleep. That comes on the night-before a race, after being knackered from the previous poor sleep.

But, unusually, on this morning I was laying there thinking that I'd had a really good, restful sleep. I was in bed by 10pm, and asleep before 10:30pm, with an almost solid night's sleep. Apart, that is, from the Fucking Cat (or Timmy, as he's sometimes known) scratching on the door at 2am to come in and sleep on the bed.

Eva starts work early on Thursdays, hence the alarm going off during the dark hours. Being somewhat more motivated by a closer departure deadline than I had, she got out of bed in a sleep haze, using the fight against gravity to help wake herself up.

I stayed in bed. There was a process, you see. She went to the bathroom, and I stayed in bed with my eyes closed hoping she'd be a very long time. She never was, and all to soon I couldn't put off getting up any longer.

Until a few months prior, I wouldn't have had to get up, but we went and acquired ourselves a Sprocker puppy that goes by the name of Rocky. And he's a an absolute lunatic. On his own, one person would be more than enough to cope, but add in five cats and an aging Labrador (although she's no trouble at all really) and pet-breakfast time really does become a two-person job.

Upstairs, Eva released the mad mutt from his crate and accompanied him out into the garden while I found some cups for coffee and tried to stop the cats from eating my feet or each other.

In a thundering clatter of doors and paws, Rat-dog (as I've ended up calling him) re-entered the hermitage, closely followed by Eva who proceeded to fill a bowl with biscuits while dog bounced around the kitchen, scattering cats in his wake on the way to be fed out in the hall, safely contained behind a closed door.

Peace. For a minute, anyway.

I fed the cats, made a couple of cups of coffee (my one a decaf, oh joy!), and we made our way to the lounge to keep an eye on Rat-dog, who'd now finished his biscuits, making sure he didn't eat anything connected to the mains. We sat there in the dark, a cup of coffee in hand, poking our phones in not-quite-awake silence.

I did the Wordle[1]. It was number 474, and the word was SLOTH. As far as omen's go, that's not a great word as you're trying to get your head around heading off for a 110-mile ultramarathon. Or, actually, maybe it's a perfect word?

Eva left at 6:30am, wishing me luck and demanding that I don't fall off a cliff. She had the air of someone who was escaping; she knew what I was like in the hour or two before leaving on one of these silly events. Bloody intolerable, that's what I'm like. Obsessed with details, one-track mind, checking and checking again. Then adjusting and checking some more.

It was lucky I didn't have anything more important to do. Like walk the puppy. And take SmallBoy to school.

I had an hour or so before I had to leave for the school run though, so I ran through my plan in my head.

---

[1] For anyone reading this book long after 2022, Wordle is an online game that's had a bit of a popularity spurt. You have to guess a 5-letter word… best to look it up on the internet (if that still exists) for more info.

This time round, I'd done very little prior preparation. For all ultramarathons I've done up to this year, I'd spent weeks working on the finer details of the plan – everything from what to take, what to leave in the car and take into the hotel room, what to pack in my race vest and drop bags, nutrition plans, timing charts, maps – all the little details sorted.

But this year, things seem to have changed. I put it down to experience, but maybe it's just laziness. Although, specifically for this particular event, it was mostly down to being ridiculously busy with work, leaving me very little time to get organised.

So, as I thought about "The Plan", it was pretty much the first time I'd put it all together in my head.

I was staying at the Duke of Wellington Wetherspoons hotel in Minehead – nothing but the finest luxury establishments for this ultrarunner! It was the same hotel I had stayed in before I started the walk on the South West Coast Path (SWCP) a little over a year before, so I knew what it was like. Anachronistic is one way of describing it. Or, maybe, just "a shithole". But at £59 for a night, cancellable up to 12pm on the day you're arriving, it was a good fit for the budget.

Not wanting to waste any money, I'd opted to book the room for 2 nights – the night before the race (Thursday), and the night it finished (Saturday). There was an obvious risk to this strategy – if I stopped early for any reason, I'd potentially be sleeping in the car on Friday night. But the risk was outweighed by the fact that having nowhere to stay on Friday night might just be the nudge I needed to keep going if things were going pear shaped. That, and it saved me sixty quid.

Having stayed before, I knew there was no parking near so had planned to park near the SWCP marker, about a 10–15-minute walk from the hotel if my memory served me correctly. This marker was both where I would be picked up by minibus the following morning, and where I would hopefully stagger back to in order to complete the race at some undetermined time after that.

So, the plan was to park up and walk to the hotel with a toothbrush, some breakfast for the morning, and everything I'd need for the race – including my drop bag. Why didn't I leave the race stuff in the car and pick it up on the way past? Mainly so I could do some last-minute fiddling in the hotel room, but also if the car got broken in to, I'd still be able to do the race if I had all my kit with me (oh, what a positive way to look at things!) I'm not sure what I'd do about leaving my car unsecured with a smashed window for a day or two while I did the race though.

At some stupid time on the Friday morning, I'd walk back to the car from the hotel, dump the clothes that I was wearing the day before into the boot of the car as I passed, leaving me just my race vest and drop bag to take on the bus.

When I finished the race, I'd walk/stagger/crawl back to the car, extract my toothbrush, clothes and any other junk I'd need for a post-ultramarathon night in a hotel room, and head back to Wetherspoons.

Once all that figuring out was done, I realised I needed a big bag to put everything in. Digging around in the cupboard I liberated one of those massive blue Ikea bags and filled it with my shoes, race vest and drop bag.

I found a big red rucksack in another cupboard, stuffed in fresh clothes for after the race (something I forget about 50% of the time, so was quite pleased I'd remembered this time), the aforementioned toothbrush, a USB power supply and some cables for charging my phone and watch, my Kindle and a bag full of race clothes. I stuffed one set of trekking poles in the side of that bag too – the second set I own was in my drop bag, as a just-in-case. It's not uncommon for people to snap carbon-fibre poles during races, so I figured I might as well take a spare pair as I've got them – better to have two pairs and only use one, than need a second and have left it in a cupboard at home.

Time rolled on, and soon I had to leave to take SmallBoy to school. Time was obviously on a hill today, as it had rolled on a little quicker than I'd been expecting, which was a bit annoying as I was supposed to have taken Rat-dog for a walk. I'd gone and got myself so involved in thinking and planning about walking back and forth between a hotel and a car and stuffing a lot of things in various bags that I ran out of time. Rat-dog would have to be walked when I got back.

For the school run, we got into the most sensible of cars – a Renault Twizy. For those of you unfamiliar, the Twizy is an electric "light quadricycle", with 2 seats (one in front of the other) and a whopping 17 horsepower. Top speed is 52mph, range is about 30-40 miles, and it costs less then £2 to fill up from flat even at today's stupidly expensive electricity prices.

Oh, and it's an absolute bloody laugh to drive! Unless you hit something – or something hits you – in which case you'll be wiped up by the next road sweeper that passes. Sounds risky, but if you drive defensively and carefully, then you'll probably survive. Kind of like a motorbike, only with a roof.

Off we shot (it's a relative term…), into all the stupid traffic you get at 8am. The queue started half a mile from home and continued on-and-off through the countless sets of roadworks over the remaining 4 miles to the school. It was worse coming back – it always is – so I was just in time to hit peak school-kids-blocking-the-road when I was trying to turn into my road. The Twizy usually gets quite a lot of attention, but today was mad – every kid in the queue seemed to be yelling that they liked the car, or "cool whip" or other such modern terms that I don't understand, but I replied with a "thank you!" to them all, under the possibly incorrect assumption that all feedback was positive. It's all a lot of fun really!

My plan was to leave for Minehead at 9am, unnecessarily early, but it would put a stop to my procrastination at home and mean that I could have a nice relaxing drive to the hotel, not being at all bothered by any hold ups, road works etc.

I took Rat-dog out for a little walk, a nice chance to get some fresh air and run through any last-minute things in my head. While walking, my glasses slipped down my nose and as I pushed them back up, I thought that it would be a good idea to take a spare pair in my drop bag – I have had glasses break on long ultramarathons in the past, and although my eyes aren't *too* bad, running 40-50 miles without glasses does make things a bit less fun than they could be. It's not like a spare pair adds much to my drop bag.

The sun was out while I was walking, but it felt surprisingly cold for 12°C, and it got me thinking that it was the right move to adjust my pack contents from what I'd used back in April.

Making that second warm layer easily accessible, so I could have it on in seconds during the night if needed, seemed very sensible.

What was a little concerning, however, was just how much my legs seemed to ache walking up the hill back home. I'd been doing a fair amount of running including lots of hills over the training, but recently I'd been tapering so all that hard work felt like it was far enough away that it shouldn't still be "in my legs". Walks over the last few days had felt good – why were my legs aching now?

The only thing I could attribute it to was maybe the lack of carbs over the last week or so as part of my preparation for the race somehow only now having an effect. The other alternative – that I was just knackered, and it was all going to go to shit when I tried to cover more than 100 miles – wasn't worth contemplating. I had another 22 hours before the race started, so I made a mental note to make sure I ate enough carbs today – maybe the 100g or so I had yesterday was a bit low.

When I got back home and into the kitchen, I had a mint "Seal" bar (Aldi's rip-off of a McVitie's Penguin bar) – it was surprisingly nice, more chocolate and a crunchier biscuit than the original, and especially nice after a week or so without any sweet things.

With SmallBoy at school, Rat-dog walked around the block, and my bag packed and repacked for the umpteenth time, I thought it was probably about time to get going. Nothing productive was going to come out of spending more time at home.

I lumped my massive box of "ultrarunning shit" into the boot of the car to cover any just-in-case scenarios that might crop up; it fitted easily and there seemed little point in kicking myself in Minehead wishing that I'd bought this or that along with me – just bring the whole bloody lot and be done with it!

My Ikea bag of race things and my red rucksack of toothbrush-and-clothes-and-chargers-and-stuff went in the boot beside the big box, and that was it. I got in the car, fired up the new Muse album, *Will of the People*, and headed in wrong direction for Minehead.

I had all day to get there, so I'd decided to take a slightly odd route to Minehead in order to grab a free charge for the car and gain myself an extra 40 miles of range, meaning that hopefully I wouldn't have to charge on the way home when I was tired after all the running. With that in mind, I headed off on a route that I was very familiar with from every time I'd visited Devon or Cornwall and set off towards Exeter.

Passing Dorchester, I stayed true to my word about eating more carbs and stopped at the palace of healthy and exquisite food that is McDonalds, grabbing myself a double sausage and egg muffin with a hash brown and Sprite (no caffeine, remember… I would much rather have had a strong black coffee!). Sat back in the car, I tucked in, thoroughly enjoying the breakfast, the only downside was having to mop the grease off my hands afterwards.

The drive onwards to Dart's Farm, just outside Exeter, was uneventful. No roadworks held me up, no unexpected queues, accidents, inclement weather, or dangerous drivers. Just a fairly pleasant, relaxed jaunt through Dorset and Devon, arriving a little after 11am, plugging the car in and setting the charge level to max.

With it having been over an hour since I last ate something and the risk of starvation growing ever more present, I bought myself a steak pasty (it's got to be done here, they're lovely!) and a decaf coffee, went back to the car and stuffed in more calories and carbs.

For reasons I've mostly forgotten, I have myself a step target of 7,500 steps a day, which I've managed for all but 2 days of the last 4-and-a-half years[2]. I was spending a good chunk of today in a car and didn't want to have to walk a few miles when I arrived at Minehead, so as the car had another 30 or 40 minutes left to charge, I took the opportunity for a wander around the fields at Dart's Farm in the sunshine. And very pleasant it was too, a walk on an undulating, gravel track, no real effort, keeping it slow and just enjoying the sounds of birds and nature (and the traffic on the M5). In the back of my mind, I couldn't help but relate the gravel track to some sections of the coast path and wondered just how different it would feel when on a very similar path tomorrow or the next day.

Back in the car I fiddled around on my phone, looking at Google Maps street view of various roads in Minehead, zooming in on the parking restrictions signs and trying to find a spot to leave the car. There was quite a selection, so I picked a road that was close to the coast path start marker but also had a direct and simple route back to the hotel, important as

---

[2] I only managed about 6,000 steps the day after the 145-mile Kennet & Avon Canal Race, but I'm letting myself off that one. And the other day, I just… forgot. I've no idea why, but I ended up around 500 steps short.

I'm not good with directions – one or two turns is about all I can cope with without technological intervention!

A quick calculation on the car satnav suggested I'd massively overestimated how much charge I'd need; it now appeared that I had more than enough to get to Minehead and back home without any risk of running low. I set the road I'd found in Minehead as the destination, unplugged the car and headed off onto roads I'd never driven on before, heading north to the Somerset coast.

3

Back to the Marker

Still Thursday, 6th October 2022

The drive to Minehead started with a stretch of the M5, but in the middle of a weekday traffic was flowing easily. When I turned off the motorway I was in countryside which reminded me of the north end of my home county of Dorset – winding roads, tall hedges and a constant smell somewhere between cowpats and strong cheese. It was twisty, slow and hilly, and, slightly worryingly, there were a lot of broken branches all over the road. The wind had been quite fierce recently and had obviously done some damage, I just hoped that it had done all it was going to do and headed off somewhere else now – I had enough to do tomorrow and Saturday without having to battle gale force winds or avoid felled trees.

Despite clear instructions on a massive satnav screen to my left, I still managed to bugger up a turn and add a mile up a hill on the wrong side of the river Exe. A quick, slightly dodgy U-turn and roll back down the hill had me back on track. Towards the end of the journey was an impressive climb up and over the Brendon Hills, passing by the highest point at Lype Hill almost 1,400ft above sea level. After the hill came some A roads, some temporary traffic lights, a couple of roundabouts and a level crossing on the steam railway, and then I was driving along the seafront at Minehead.

I arrived at the road I'd picked out back at Dart's Farm, found a reasonable looking spot to leave a car for 2-and-a-half days, then went for a gentle wander down to the seafront to stretch my legs and soak up some atmosphere.

It was wonderfully reminiscent, bringing back strong memories of a year before when I'd started from here in an attempt to walk the whole of the South West Coast Path. I stood for a moment, contemplating the huge task that was ahead of me tomorrow, an epic journey that – if all went well – would see me arrive back here, exhausted but elated, in a bit over 2 days' time.

Most UK long distance paths have some sort of marker at the ends, and the one in Minehead is pretty decent as markers go. Designed by A-level student Sarah Ward, her entry winning the contest, and sculpted by Owen Cunningham, it was erected in 2001 and depicts two giant hands holding an unfolded map. The galvanised steel construction stands about 8 or 9 feet tall, and despite hiding behind trees from the road side, it's a dominant but pleasant looking piece on the seafront promenade.

Respects paid to the marker, I took a photo with my phone and lobbed it in the direction of Instagram, then stood for a minute staring out to sea at Hinckley Point nuclear power station.

I've been fascinated with nuclear power since I was a kid and used to occasionally visit the research site at Winfrith, about 10 miles from where I grew up, to go on the tour of the reactor buildings. The Winfrith ones are all closed down now, but

Hinkley Point is... well... it's mostly closed down too. For now, at least. Hinkley Point A – an old school Magnox reactor – ran from 1965 through to 2000, and Hinkley Point B – a newer Advanced Gas-cooled Reactor (but still quite old design by today's standards) – has just been switched off in August 2022 after 45 years of electricity generation. Hinkley Point C – a name which may sound familiar – is under construction. It's running a couple of years late, with a planned commissioning date of mid-2027, and is a mere £12 or £13 billion over budget. Hmmm, that's going well then!

Sightseeing done, I wandered back to the car, got my big Ikea bag and rucksack out the boot and headed off down to the main street through Minehead towards the hotel.

On the drive over, I'd been thinking about whether I'd forgotten anything. The only thing I could come up with was some water for the morning, the bit between leaving the hotel and starting the race. With my pre-race nutrition strategy involving very minimal carbohydrate on race day until an hour into the race, I had a perfectly normal breakfast in the form of a tin of mackerel, a tin of corned beef, a tin of steak pie filling, a lump of Parmesan and a bag of salted cashews... everyone has that for breakfast, right? But I hadn't bought anything to drink, and I didn't want to not have anything between leaving the hotel at 4-something in the morning and starting the race at 7:30am. So, the plan was to call by the Co-op on the high street and buy a bottle of water that I could have with me on the bus and make sure I was nicely hydrated when I started running.

I arrived at the hotel – via the Co-op – about 15 minutes after leaving the car, so I reckoned it would take less than that to get back tomorrow, even with a quick stop at the car to drop off my rucksack. I thought it best to aim for 4:45am at the pick-up point to give me a 15-minute safety net, and that meant an alarm for… eeek… 3:30am. Lovely.

I checked in to the hotel and found my way to room 107, with its single bed, peeling wallpaper and damp patches in the bathroom. It wasn't luxury, but I really couldn't have cared less – it had a bed, a bath/shower and somewhere to get food downstairs, that was all I needed.

With no-one else coming into the room between now and me leaving in the morning, I unpacked and laid all my race gear out on the floor in the order in which I'd need it: shoes, gaiters, socks, calf guards, pants, compression shorts, over shorts, long sleeved merino top, hat, race vest, poles. Nothing seemed to be missing, which was a bit of a relief.

I laid out my odd breakfast on the desk, the collection of different shaped tins creating a mini cityscape on the tray next to the kettle. I noticed a pack of chocolate cookies on the tray, and within 30 seconds there were no more chocolate cookies on the tray. There were only 2 in the pack, but I still made them disappear impressively fast.

The plan was to have an early night, ideally in bed by around 7pm. I wasn't expecting to go to sleep very quickly, but figured just lying down, reading, or listening to a podcast was resting and good preparation for tomorrow. I'd done all of my 7,500 steps for the day, so I didn't have to go out again, and took up residence on the bed despite it only being 3:30pm.

I lay and read my book for a while, my eyes drifting close despite the early hour, which I hoped was a good sign for maybe, just maybe, falling asleep easily. I managed to hang around in the room until 5:30pm, then decided that was late enough and headed to the pub downstairs for dinner.

I'd read the first few chapters of my *Half the Path* book a few days before to remind myself what was coming (even though that was in the other direction, it was still quite helpful!). One of the things that stood out was the food that I'd had in this very pub the night before the walk. It had sounded good, so I opted for the same again: a pint of Guinness, a sirloin steak and a jacket potato with a side of halloumi fries.

I polished off the steak, the potato, all the millions of peas and the Guinness, still wondering when the halloumi fries might turn up. I went to the bar to chase them up and ended up with a desert of cold halloumi fries… not as nice as they could have been, but I still quite enjoyed them.

While sat at the table eating, I had my iPad and was researching places to look out for on the route. I've written 3 books about walks or runs I've done on the South West Coast Path, and for each one I've learnt the most about the areas when researching *after* the event. This time, I'd already done about 90% of the route so had a good idea of what to look out for, but I spent a bit of time over dinner looking at the other 10%.

The two points that stood out were Hartland Point Lighthouse (I love a good lighthouse!), and Titchbury Radar Station which, on looking at pictures, bought back memories of a trip out with the family years before. We'd parked in a car park and gone for a walk in rolling green hills, in the distance stood an odd concrete post with what looked like a giant white golf ball on the top. On that walk I took a photo of all of us sat on a hill which we had on our lounge wall for years and I couldn't remember where it had been taken... now I knew!

Back up in the room, I re-organised my kit for the 18th time to make sure I had everything ready to go, then packed the stuff that I wouldn't need for the race into my big rucksack ready to dump into the boot of the car.

Last thing, I did my usual filling of soft flasks the night before so I could leave them on the side and make sure they didn't leak. As I put them on the windowsill of the bathroom, I noticed one was a little limp, and a bit more inspection found a tiny hole in the side, an almost invisible spray of water escaping when squeezed.

A moment of panic rose at the thought of having only one water bottle for the 20-plus mile gaps between aid stations – that wasn't going to work! The feeling quickly turned to excitement as I remembered the spare soft flask I'd put in my race vest, so I filled it and checked it wasn't leaking. Yes! Vindicated! There *was* a point to bringing all that spare shite with me... finally!

But now that I'd used my spare flask, I didn't have a spare for the actual run tomorrow. Not to worry, I didn't usually carry a spare with me, although I'd just proven that the spare was useful... hopefully I wouldn't need *another* spare one. Then it dawned on me: I had my "big box of ultra-running shit" in the boot of the car, which included a few spares soft flasks. Double vindicated (is that a phrase?) – from now on, I'm always going to bring everything with me when I do an ultra!

All of the organisational nonsense done, I had a shower in anticipation of just how disgustingly stinky I was going to get over the next 48 hours, then got into bed before 8pm.

I phoned Eva, had a bit of a pre-"I'm doing stupid shit" chat, read a book for a bit, then put on a podcast.

One of the less-delightful things about the Duke of Wellington hotel is that outside the window of the rooms is a noisy fan. A very, very noisy fan. I don't know what the hell it does, but it doesn't sound too far from a jet engine readying for take-off. Although noisy, it's a very white noise – like a waterfall or static – and it does serve to block the myriad sounds that might come from a pub during the evening. Despite the fan noise, I managed to fall asleep surprisingly rapidly, at a little after 8pm.

You may then expect that I'd sleep all the way through the night, but instead I woke quite a few times, each time nervously checking my watch to see how much longer I had to rest, how many more hours or minutes I could stay lying down, in the dark, in bed, until I had to get up and race. The watch first told me it 9:50pm, then 11:50pm, then 2:20pm and then…

4

Has anyone got a map?

Friday, 7th October 2022

… 3:12am. I thought about trying to go back to sleep, but… 18 minutes. What's the point? I lay there thinking about the scary but exciting adventure I was about to embark on, and what I needed to do after getting out of bed. At 3:25am, I turned on the bedside light, stretched and got up.

There's an excitement and a nervousness when you get out of bed on race day. It's the first step of something really big, a journey into the unknown – even for a race you've done before. A kind of "no going back now" moment; up until now, it's been something in the future, now it's time to actually get on with it.

First up, a hot drink, something which always kick-starts the day for me, even if it doesn't have any caffeine in. I'd already filled the kettle up before going to bed with enough water for a cup of something, so I flicked the switch for it to boil.

Next up, food. I can't say I was entirely looking forward to my very odd breakfast, but I knew getting in a load of calories now was important as I'm usually a bit crap at eating during races. With some trepidation, I got started with the steak pie filling, opening up the tin and using my Tifoon[3] to mouth a couple of spoonfuls. I was in the dark bathroom, keeping the light off as I didn't really want to see what it looked like, and leaning over the sink just in case it tasted absolutely disgusting and I needed to abort in a hurry. The taste wasn't actually too bad, but the texture was a bit questionable. Half the tin was enough, I tipped the rest down the toilet, washed out the can and got myself a glass of water to wash the gristly bits of beef, horse, unicorn and whatever else is in that stuff.

Next, back in the light of the room, I tore off the top of the pack of cheese. I do like Parmesan, but I've never had it within about 10 minutes of waking up, and my head and stomach weren't really in the mood. A small chunk was all I could manage.

Corned beef. I haven't had corned beef for... oooh, at least 20 years. It's the only food I know of that comes in a tin with a key to open it. As I tried to get my tragically bitten fingernails under the spot-welded key, I did contemplate just why corned beef was pretty much unique in having this strange opening mechanism. It seems corned beef was originally supplied to the military, and being all about practicality, they liked the square can design as it's more efficiently packed into cartons. The problem with a square can is those tight corners make it a nuisance to open with a tin opener, so some bright spark came up with the key idea. In this current age of pull tabs on cans, it seems the classic corned-beef tin design is now primarily

---

[3] You've heard of a spork, right? (A portmanteau of spoon and fork if you haven't). Well, just to be a bit quirky, the British company Alpkit sell a titanium version, which they call a *Tifoon*, a mix of titanium, fork and spoon.

hanging on for marketing reasons, keeping it distinctive on a shelf.

I got the key onto the little metal tab, gave it a twist, and as it took up the tension in a way that suggested something might snap leaving me with an unopenable tin, I mentally crossed my fingers. Moments later, the tin was open, and I had a wodge of fatty beef standing in front of me on the desk. Corned. What the hell does that mean? OK… actually, I don't want to know. I got my Tifoon out and tucked in. It was… tolerable. And fatty. Lots of calories. I managed to get about half of it eaten, then gave up.

The kettle had boiled, so I tipped some hot water out into a cup. I toyed with the idea of just drinking the hot water – you can't get much more caffeine-free than that – but opted instead for showing it a teabag for about half a second, then flooding it with milk. Minimal caffeine, minimal flavour, but a nice indication to my sleepy body that it was probably time to start preparing for the day.

For the last 4 or more years, I've worn the same shoes and socks for every ultra – Saucony Peregrine shoes, a pair of Injinji toe-socks on my feet, and then a pair of Drymax socks over the top. Actually, I tell a lie – for the flat, non-technical Kennet & Avon Canal race, I wore Altra Paradigm road shoes, but kept the same double-sock system.

Not this time, though. At least 3 of the runs I've done over those years have ended up with my feet trapped in soaking socks for hours, creating something pretty close to trench-foot. Also, the Peregrines are OK for rough terrain, but I didn't want to run 30 miles on a flat tarmac cycle path in them.

One of the things about doing these long races with no crew is you have to try and pick a shoe that works for the whole distance. If you've got someone meeting you at various places, you can swap to road shoes for flat sections, meaty trail shoes for muddy bits, and comfortable in-between shoes for others. But without crew, you need a do-it-all shoe. And those don't really exist – you have to compromise something.

This time round, I'd gone with Altra Lone Peak 6 shoes, and a single pair of Darn Tough Hiker socks, neither of which I'd worn for an ultramarathon before.

Here's my reasoning. Both the Lone Peaks and the socks worked well for me on the walk last year – including on the same stretch covered on the North Coast 110 race - and I'd be doing a lot of walking. The shoes were comfortable on all but the rockiest of terrain, had fair grip as long as I wasn't on wet rocks and were lightweight. The socks hadn't caused any issues walking either, and what's more it was a damn sight easier changing one pair of normal socks than two pairs, one of them being fiddly toe-socks.

Zero drop shoes and untested socks? I was beginning to sound like Pat Robbins who often goes out and does big events in untested gear... it seems to work OK for him, fingers crossed I'd get the same luck!

I did the usual slathering of greasy Squirrels Nut Butter over 80% of my body between the top of my hips and the top of my legs, twanged on my delightfully attractive anti-chafe undercrackers, and then squeezed myself into my compression shorts. I did a pretty convincing attempt at a New Zealand

Haka in order to shift everything into the right place, then got to work on the bottom end of my legs.

Calf guards slithered up my legs, gaiters on my ankles, a sprinkling of 2Toms Blistershield powder into my socks, then those onto my feet. And what a revelation! Normally, I'm fighting with getting my toes into the little toe-pockets of my Injinji socks at this time, but with these I just slipped them on like a… well, like a *normal* pair of socks. Which was important, as I did intend to change them later in the race, and not having to fight with two toes trying to get into the same little toe-pocket would be a big help. Shoes on – those Lone Peaks are quite soft and flexible, so they were easy to get into – I clipped the gaiters on…

Oh Altra, why did you change the way gaiters attach? On the Lone Peak 4's and 5's, there's a little metal loop that gaiters hook in to, and it works really well. On the 6's – which is what I had – they routed the flat shoe lace through a little channel at the base of the laces, so, in theory, you have the perfect spot to clip on gaiters.

Genius, huh?

No. It doesn't bloody work. As soon as the laces curl just a tiny bit – and they will after a run or two – I just could *not* get the gaiters clipped on! Luckily, I knew this was likely to happen as it had several times during my training, and I'd run with the gaiters clipped on to the lower laces (rather than that special tiny strip at the bottom) and that seemed to work OK, not digging into my foot or coming loose. After one quick failed attempt at attaching them in the intended way, I just clipped them on to a random bit of lace on the shoe and hoped it would hold out. Shoe manufacturers keep fiddling with proven designs, I'm not the only one who wishes they'd just leave the bloody things alone!

I'd been thinking about the changed I had made in relation to my warm tops, making sure the new idea of having two in my pack, one easily accessible, was still a good idea. Checking the weather, it was still at a minimum of 11°C for the whole duration of the race, so I opted for wearing one of the long-sleeved tops and sticking an identical one into my emergency drybag, removing the thicker thermal one that was in there originally. Even dropping the temperature down a bit for night time and slow movement, it should still be comfortably warm in a long-sleeved top and coat.

Well, that was just about it then. I had my massive blue Ikea bag with fully loaded race vest complete with poles, drop bag, and a Tesco bag-for-life with a partly emptied 2 litre bottle of water to save weight and some cashew nuts. I figured sitting on a minibus eating corned beef, Parmesan or tinned mackerel would get me forcefully ejected from said minibus pronto, so I carefully put the remains of that lot into the standard teeny tiny hotel-room bin in such a way that I hoped nothing would leak out and cause any mess.

My walk from the car yesterday had deliberately been a little extended, to soak up the atmosphere of Minehead and to call past the Co-op, so I had a quick look on my phone and double-checked the most direct route to the car. Out the hotel, along The Parade a little way towards the seafront, left up Blenheim Road and then just before I get to the coast, turn into the road with my car on – simple enough that even I could probably do that without buggering it up. Ten minutes tops, 15 with a bit of faffing at the car, so I planned to leave at 4:30am.

I stood in the room, wondering what to do. It was only twenty-past four, but there really wasn't any point in hanging around nervously tapping my feet and biting my nails, so I stuck on my warm blue waterproof coat assuming it would be at least a little chilly at this time of the morning. With the big rucksack on my back, and the surprisingly heavy blue Ikea bag tipping me to one side as I tried to quietly close the door, I headed along the corridor and down the stairs.

A guy was at the bottom doing whatever needed doing in a hotel at four-twenty-something in the morning, and he walked with me to the front door to let me out. We had a little chat about the front door being awkward, and he had to give it a decent couple of shoves to release it and free me into the Somerset morning.

Unsurprisingly, no one was about. It's always a bit of a surreal and quite nice feeling, having a town to yourself. I plodded my way up the wide road of the Parade, spotted the very obvious turn to Blenheim Road and headed left, trying to walk as slowly as I could to waste the extra time I'd gained by leaving the room 10 minutes earlier than planned.

Blenheim Gardens passed by on the right, a lovely green area in the town by daytime, but an ominous blackness behind a line of trees during the night. At a junction, I took a slight left, and moments later I was at the car.

I unlocked the boot and dumped in the red rucksack and blue Ikea bag. I clicked open my big-box-of-ultrarunning-shit and fished around for a spare soft-flask. I picked up my race vest, drop bag and carrier bag with water & nuts, as well as the freshly liberated soft flask, closed the boot, and headed a short distance down the road.

A little way away from the car so as not to advertise the fact I'd be leaving it for a day or two, I put the spare soft flask and my car key in the back of my race vest, swung it round on to my back, and started wandering down towards the seafront.

Fairly typically for me, I was the first person to arrive. It was 4:35am, not a popular time to be wandering along Minehead seafront. I walked past the dark and shadowy Quay Hotel, which was mentioned in the pick-up instructions, but as I had plenty of time I thought I'd slowly drift the 100 metres or so down to coast path marker.

It was damp in the air, not really raining, but not completely dry. The visibility was decent though, and the lights of Hinkley Point C construction site glowed out from their isolated spot on the horizon. I passed a little seafront shelter, then reached the marker, standing in front, again lost in contemplation. Just a carefully crafted lump of galvanised steel, the marker holds a lot of meaning for me, with my slightly unnatural obsession with the South West Coast Path. Every time I'm near it, a whole flood of memories come back to me – the races, the walks, the camping, the *adventures*. As well as the reverie, today I was also thinking about what was coming, the adventure I was about to embark on.

A figure appeared from the darkness, a bag in one hand and a race vest on her back. We chatted a little as we walked back towards the Quay Hotel, and then she went on to drop some stuff off in her car.

While I was lingering around a bench opposite the hotel, a couple of guys appeared, and a few minutes later there was a group of 6 or 7 of us chatting a bit about the weather, races we'd done… all the usual nonsense you do when you're British, nervous, and stood on a seafront before 5am.

I wandered back over to the sea wall and just stood, looking out, concentrating a little on taking slow, deep breaths to stay as calm as I could while looking across the lights of the town and the coast in an attempt to dissipate the moments of panic that rose up in me.

The bright lights of Butlins shone out like search lights on a prison or military camp. The sea gently lapped at the other side of the wall I was leaning against. The group behind me chattered on. And I breathed in. And out. In. And out.

"I reckon this is us," said one of the people behind me as a pair of headlights accompanied by the sound of a lumpy diesel engine headed towards us, drove a little past, and proceeded to do a fairly awkward multi-point turn in the road while several people in the group commented about there being a roundabout a few metres further on.

The minibus pulled up on the kerbside adjacent to where we were all lingering, and we tentatively headed over. I assumed it would be one of the Climb South West crew doing the driving in a hired minibus, as, I think, did everyone else. So, we all just stood there, waiting for the driver to jump down and give us a cheery greeting, mentioning what a bunch of idiots we all were etc. etc.

But no. The guy just sat in the driver's seat, looking over at us. And we just stood there, looking over at him.

Thankfully, someone on our team had some initiative, and after a few seconds strolled over to open the door.

"Are you for us?" said the guy who opened the door.

"Er…" was the response, at which point we all just got in. The driver hadn't said no, and there was unlikely to be a Scenic Tour of Devon and Somerset heading off two hours before sunrise.

It was a 16-seater I think, and as there weren't that many of us there was enough space for one person per row of seats. We all climbed in and settled down.

"Anyone got a preference for the route?" asked the driver, which seemed a bit of an odd question. Surely he was the one who should know how to get where we're going, and what the best route was.

After a few quietly mumbled "no"s, someone asked how long it would be. "An hour and 45 minutes" was the reply.

That's quite a long drive… especially if you consider that we were getting turfed out at the other end and had to run back to where we were now!

It was 5am. We'd be there around 6:45am, giving us a nice chunk of time to get organised – kit check, trackers, numbers, toilet etc, nice and ready to get going at 7:30am.

Oh, wouldn't that have been nice…

5

Stopping service from Minehead to Hartland Quay

Friday, 7th October, 05:30

An hour and forty-five minutes is a nice length of time to travel. Not long enough to get really bored of the journey, but long enough that you can relax without feeling like you're just about to arrive.

As we started off, I did some general fiddling about: drank some water, ate some cashews, put a seatbelt around my dropbag and race vest so if I fell asleep, they wouldn't fly down the bus in the event of heavy braking, that sort of thing. Then I closed my eyes and pretended there was a snowball's chance in hell of me getting some sleep on a moving vehicle.

It was mostly quiet on the bus, except for one point where someone took a phone call and was speaking really quite loudly, although I wasn't paying much attention to what they were saying. It sounded like someone at the back of the bus, and although it seemed unnecessarily loud, it didn't really bother me as we were in a diesel bus caning it along some windy country roads – the background noise wasn't exactly quiet.

Five minutes later, someone else was on the phone, also talking loudly. And, strangely in exactly the same voice. My brain fuzzed into action and resolved that it was, in fact, the same person. I was beginning to gather the gist of the conversation, and it sounded like someone had missed the bus.

The tone of the engine changed as it struggled up a hill, and a few down-shifts suggested this was quite a steep one. It was at this point that Steve, the guy on the phone, asked the driver if there was any chance we could go back and pick a guy up who'd been left behind.

"No!" came a half laughed, somewhat incredulous response. "We're 20 minutes out of Minehead, so if we turn around now it'll add at least 40 minutes and there's no chance we'll make it in time."

I would have given up at this point. Bad luck to Andy Quicke, the guy who'd missed the bus, but we did leave on time and the instructions were pretty clear. Sometimes it just not meant to be.

But, instead of me on the end of the phone, Andy had Steve. And Steve wasn't going to give up. He suggested to Andy that he get in his car and catch us up. I wasn't quite sure how he was going to do that, as the minibus driver appeared to have a day-job as a Formula One driver, but the plan was in place and Andy had set off. The poor bugger was now beginning his first of 2 races of the day!

There was some looking at maps on screens while fighting with Exmoor mobile phone reception, and the plan was made to meet at Lynmouth, a little under 20 miles from Minehead. After Steve hung up from Andy, the driver helpfully pointed out that we weren't going through Lynmouth, and we'd have to make a detour to get there. This then sparked another conversation between Steve and the driver, which ended up with a plan to stop at Barnstaple instead – about 35 miles from

Minehead – as there was more likely to be parking places and we wouldn't have to detour. Steve tried to make contact with Andy to direct him to Barnstaple.

As I looked out the window, we passed a "Welcome to Lynmouth" sign. I was beginning to have my doubts about this driver.

The driver stopped on the road next to what people suggested was a big car park but looked to me to be the same blackness as everywhere else I could see.

Steve got out the minibus in an attempt to get better reception to be able to call Andy, although a quick glance at my phone showed lots of signal bars, suggesting it was likely to be Andy who was in the crappy signal area.

At that moment, the heavens decided to dump a shit-ton of rain on us – or, more specifically, on the minibus. And Steve, who was still outside trying to get signal and make sure that Andy didn't go to Barnstaple but instead headed here.

I was having some pretty selfish feelings right about now. It was 5:50am. My stress levels were going up, the nice calm and relaxing buffer of time we had on arrival at Hartland Quay was evaporating, and we'd end up having to rush through all the administration stuff and then get going immediately.

My brain carried on with its panicked thoughts. We'd tried. Well, technically, *Steve* had tried – the rest of us had just sat on a bus. But some things weren't meant to be. Let's just get going and we could dedicate our runs to Andy or something. Whatever… time to go now.

The door opened, and Steve got back in the van. He was soaking wet, and yet he was still trying to sort Andy out. I was getting the sense he was a thoroughly nice bloke! He hadn't successfully got through to Andy though, so we were just going to sit and wait for some indeterminate amount of time until he either turned up or we got so late that there was no option but to get going.

After another 5 minutes, at just around 6am, I piped up that maybe we should ask the race director (RD) what they thought. I wasn't trying to spanner the situation with Andy, in fact I was beginning to get a bit invested in it. We'd waited for long enough it seemed a shame to give up now! But also, it wasn't really our decision to make. There were 10 or so people on the bus, and at least that many waiting at Hartland Quay for the start in an hour or so's time – we needed someone in charge to make a decision about when to call it a day.

It turns out it was the RD that had got in touch with Steve about Andy, so he was up to speed on the situation. And at that moment, a set of headlights appeared from behind us driving like Mansell on a good day and drew up next to the minibus.

He'd made it!

At least to a road in Lynmouth. The small matter of where to dump your car for 48 hours in a little coastal Devon town without getting towed, clamped or having to take out a second mortgage was yet to be solved.

After a brief chat through the front window, the headlights disappeared off down a road towards the sea and continued a surprising distance further before disappearing around a corner. A minute or two later, we all decided it might be nice to go down after him. He was probably used to running considering what we were all about to do, but there was no sense in making him do another unnecessary half a mile back up from the seafront.

Down at the front, past the bottom of the world's tallest water-driven funicular railway, we waited by the entrance to a car park while Andy fed the meter.

Long enough later to have us concerned, he appeared at the door. The machine was out-of-order, not taking money, so he'd left a note in the window. Brave guy. This run, which was already fairly pricey, could be about to cost him a whole lot more if the traffic wardens round here were grumpy.

At 6:10am, we head off from Lynmouth, about 30 minutes behind schedule at this point, but potentially a chunk more as the traffic was likely to grow and slow us further through the towns as we approached Friday rush hour.

And as predicted, as the sky began to lighten, Barnstaple was notable for the increase in traffic. It wasn't heavy, but if it were still dark, the route would have been clearer. And we were still over 25 miles away from the start.

I munched nervously on a few more cashews, suddenly having the thought of whether anyone on the bus was allergic to nuts! I thought for a moment, decided no-one had said anything and if anyone had a serious allergy they probably would have mentioned it, but I closed up the bag of nuts anyway just to be on the safe side. Most of the bag had gone anyway, I'd probably had more than enough.

We passed Clovelly on the route to Hartland Point… which, with my crap sense of direction, didn't seem like quite the right way to go. Not the Clovelly bit – that seemed sensible – but Hartland Point was about 3 miles north of the start and surely there was more direct route to Hartland Quay?

A few more turns, all heading to "Point" rather than "Quay", and we reached a dead end at a farm, much to the consternation of the driver.

"There's the hotel," he said, pointing south down the coast. "I just don't know how to get there."

It was 7:20am. The race was supposed to start in 10 minutes, and we had no idea how the hell to get to the start.

The most obvious route was signposted "Unsuitable for Motor Vehicles", but he gave it a go anyway. It turned out to be unsuitable for motor vehicles, so we reversed back up to the top.

Someone on the bus suggested that there might have been a sign to Hartland Quay a few hundred metres back up the road, and a others chimed up in agreement, so we rapidly headed off back up the single-track road with no more guidance from the technology on the dashboard.

A minute or two later, we took a left turn and a moment after that half the bus yelled out that we'd gone the wrong way. A quick application of brakes, selection of reverse gear, and, using the advantage that 7am brings you on narrow country roads, a swift backtrack through a junction to take the right route posted to Hartland Quay.

A mile or two further down the windy road and as we headed down towards the coast, a guy was out on the road waving and pointing down the hill.

We continued down, round a corner and into a car park. The car park was empty of cars but had a single boat laying on the grass near the entrance. Being devoid of both cars and people, it didn't look like the start point of a race.

A quick three-point turn in the car park, then we were back out on the road continuing down the hill and into the correct, busier car park for the Hartland Quay Hotel, swerving between cars and people in a way that had me moderately nervous about wiping out a few competitors. The brakes brought us to a standstill, and at just about 7:30am, we had finally made it!

Despite the location being less than ideal, Hartland Quay has a history as a harbour that dates back to the time of Henry VII. The authorisation for the construction of the harbour was passed with an Act of Parliament in 1566, sponsored by a few notable chaps including Sir Walter Raleigh and Sir Francis Drake. It was built towards the end of the 16th century, and heavy goods like lime, slate and coal were shipped in, with barley and oats being shipped out. But the location meant that was in constant need of repair due to the fierceness of the sea. The arrival of the railway in Bideford in the second half of the 19th century meant the pier was left unmaintained, and a massive storm in 1887 finally washed it away, leaving just remnants visible at low tide. The slipway that's currently visible was constructed in 1970 for pleasure use by members of the Hartland Boat Club.

The buildings were repurposed, the malthouse and stables becoming 'The Wrecker's Retreat' bar, and the old Customs House becoming the hotel whose car park in which a bunch of runners were currently alighting from a minibus.

The race was due to start pretty much now. But minor details like that shouldn't get in the way of a kit check (and, although I sound sarcastic, they really shouldn't). Justin and the team of Climb South West crew were efficient and organised, obviously somewhat thrown by the late arrival, but working through what needed to be done in a quick but concise and careful manner.

Kit check consisted of showing our survival bag, head torch and waterproof jacket – probably the 3 most essential things should things go awry on the coast path in the middle of the night.

We got our numbers, had a tracker taped to the shoulder strap of our packs, and I dumped my drop back in the back of a van after double checking it was the right one, then headed to the toilet quickly, not wanting to reappear sometime after the race had started!

I returned to find the pre-race briefing underway and headed to the main table to get some safety pins so I could attach the number to my shorts. It didn't occur to me that I was standing just behind Justin, who was giving the briefing, and that put me in full view of everyone waiting to start the race.

Now, I have a history of making a meal of pinning my number on. And today, it was outdoors and windy, meaning there was no chance it would go right.

Somehow, it went perfectly. 4 safety pins, straight in, number on relatively straight and flat, no impromptu injections from a rusty needle. Maybe I need an audience every time? This was a good omen!

Although the wind was strong and gusty, it was actually quite warm, so the last thing I did was take off my blue coat and shove it in the back of my race vest, which I then donned and clipped up ready to go.

I picked up my walking poles, extended them and clipped them together, finishing just in time to hear Justin mention the intimidating looking cliffs that would start us off.

And by Jove, they were. I looked north, and there was a sawtooth set of hills, ominously shrouded in sea-spray under the weak early morning sunlight.

The briefing ended with a suggestion that we shouldn't fall off any cliffs, and that some of them were potentially quite falloffable. And that there was someone first-aid trained at every checkpoint. Ah, great. They can sort me out if I fall off the cliff then.

The group of runners headed from the car park over to the bottom of the steep road we'd driven down in the bus about 20 minutes before, to a flag marking the start, a point 110 miles of coast path away from Minehead.

Justin went part way up the hill and took a couple of photos on his phone. A quick look at his watch, and he shouted down "I'll start you at 7:56."

Thirty seconds of waiting in the wind can seem a long time. Especially before more than one hundred miles of racing. It seemed to drag on forever, the time ticking slowly towards the next minute.

And then...

"Go!"

6

The new bit

Race Start: 7th October 2022, 07:56

Of the 21 starters, I'd say 80% of us started running up the steep hill – myself included – before we quickly remembered that we were in an ultramarathon, had 110 miles to go, and were running up a steep hill. The majority of us dropped back to a walk for the rest of the short road section, round a corner and onto a track signposted with an acorn indicating the route of the South West Coast Path.

A little way along the track, the path met the road again at Rocket House, a lovely looking house with stunning views out to sea, and now, as a lot of historical buildings in this area are, available to let should you be interested.

The lethal fingers of rock that head out under the surface of the sea at Hartland have been responsible for many, many shipwrecks. After the tragic loss of 18 of the 28 crew when the 2,203-ton steamship SS Uppingham was wrecked in November 1890, the *Hartland Life Saving Apparatus Company* was formed, and the Rocket Apparatus House built to house the equipment invented by Cornishman Henry Trengrouse. I've mentioned Trengrouse before in *Buckle Up*, when he witnessed a tragic shipwreck near Loe Bar in south Cornwall and came up with the idea of using a rocket to fire a rescue line to a ship in distress. Well, here atop the cliffs of Hartland Quay, was one such deployment of his invention.

The coast path headed through a gate, past the front of the house and out onto rolling open grassland heading north, the scary looking clifftops and valleys ominously present ahead.

The last few ultras I've done have had fields of over 100 competitors, and the starts have been busy affairs, especially when the trails got narrow. The Arc of Attrition, for example, has so many people starting that you're almost in a queue for the first few miles.

This race immediately felt different. Less than half a mile in, at the first gate, we were dispersed enough to be going through one at a time, with enough gap for the gate to clack closed between runners.

This was something I'd been looking forward to. I'm an antisocial bugger at the best of times, and I was looking forward to having some big chunks of time on my own for this race.

The track went directly north across The Warren, with Eye Cove on the left. I was running across the exact area where, back in 2010, Jeremy Clarkson's Citroen CX derived motorhome 'accidentally' went over the cliff and smashed on the beach below during a Top Gear[4] episode.

The coast path here was discernible as a slightly flattened strip in the grass, and just off the track to the right was an unusual shaped brick building, or rather the remnants of one. At first, I thought it might have been a church, but the red

---

[4] Series 15, Episode 4 of Top Gear, if you're wondering. It was quite an amusing one, if you like that sort of thing.

brick didn't really fit, and the stupendously high arches looked more like the entrance to a castle. A teeny, tiny castle though.

It's actually the ruins of a folly called *The Pleasure House*, which sounds a lot seedier (at least in my mind) than it actually was. It's thought to have originally been built in the 16th century, then remodelled in the 18th century, most likely used as a nice place to have a picnic. As you would likely have arrived in a horse-drawn carriage, the height of the arches made a bit more sense.

Round a corner, I came to the first of the valleys, a dusty, stony path descending down to the Abbey River. The valley sides were tree-lined, the lower section grassy with a single white house visible by the water. At the head of the valley, just poking above the treeline, was the top of the tower of St Nectan's church, colloquially known as the "Cathedral of North Devon".

Being less than a mile into the race, I hadn't really warmed up yet, so I was taking it relatively cautiously on the descent. There were enough lumps of rock and large cracks on the path that it would be fairly easy to take a tumble, and I really didn't want that at any point, let along this early in the race.

I might as well have been standing still, though, as Emma Brock came past me in a bright pink t-shirt. I thought I was average, maybe just heading into 'ok' at descending, but she was absolutely flying down the hill! I did think to myself that maybe she was pushing a little hard this early on…

Although while moving we were generally quite spaced apart, at certain points where the pace dropped we clumped together and right now I was ending up with a collection of people closing in behind. It seems like my descending on mildly technical terrain wasn't up to much at all and I was starting to hold people up behind, which in turn made me push on a little harder than I really wanted to.

The same happened on the uphill, and by the time I crested the top of the first decent hill I was a bit puffed out, which was not the plan within the first 1% of the race. As soon as the path ahead widened out, I pulled over to one side and let people pass by, determined to keep my effort level down.

One guy in front of me had stopped to take a picture of the bay below, and as I got closer to the edge of the cliff to see over, I realised why. The view down over Blegberry Beach was spectacular. The tide was out, and the black rocks of the bay ran in ridged lines out from the base of the cliff, looking like a giant had taken a huge rake to the stone. This extended out to sea under the water, and it was easy to see how treacherous the area would be for marine vessels getting remotely close to the shore.

Both the view and the chap taking the photo reminded me that, prior to starting, I'd decided to break form and take lots of photos. It was a long race; a few seconds here and there wouldn't make any difference to the end result, but I'd have lots of images to look back at. However, in that moment, only a mile or so in, I just wanted to get on with moving. I figured I'd take photos later - after all, there was plenty more to come.

The rocks below were part of a fantastic area of interesting geology. Hartland Quay and the surround area has some amazing structures, especially the winding, curving strata of rock that make up the cliffs, but that meant a lot of the interesting bits were only visible from the shore. It's another place I've added to the long list of South West Coast Path locations to go back and visit, dropping down the water level to take a proper look at formations in slow time, rather than racing past on top of the cliffs.

A little over half an hour after leaving that hotel car park, the bright white structure of Hartland Point lighthouse was visible, standing out against the blue sea and black rocks.

Now, this was one of the things I'd been reading about while munching steak and potato the previous night, so I was freshly versed on a little of its history. Originally built in 1874, the tower is 18 metres tall, the lamp 37 metres above sea level, and it could be seen at a distance of around 25 miles. Interestingly, the signal was a mix of white and red flashes, the red being created by panels of ruby glass which is made by mixing gold with glass during the production process, making it even more valuable than your common garden lighthouse optic.

The currents in this area are so fierce that the Roman's use to call this point 'The Promontory of Hercules', and the lighthouse was constantly battered by the heavy seas. To protect it, rocks were broken from the cliff and piled up on the beach, but each time there was a combination of north-westerly gales and high spring tide, the rocks were washed away. Eventually, in 1925, a protective wall was constructed, 30 metres long and 6 metres high.

There's been a fair amount of change at the lighthouse. Electrification came along in 1927, with the original optic being replaced by one which generated 6 quick white flashes instead of the red/white combo of the previous one. By 1984, it was fully automatic, and the keeper's cottage was demolished to build a helipad, required as the access road kept getting blocked by rock falls and land slips.

Just as the first decade of the 21st century finished, Trinity House reviewed the light requirements at this location and determined that only 8 nautical miles was needed, which could be met with a modern solar-powered LED beacon mounted on the cliff in front of the original structure.

And so, Hartland Point lighthouse became a former lighthouse, and was marketed for £500,000. And for that, you get yourself a 3-bedroom accommodation set over two storeys, lots of stores, a helipad, and 16 acres of ground, along with "the best sea views in the area!" As lovely as it sounds, I'd imagine the upkeep is quite considerable! And I think I'd be pretty safe placing a bet that Tesco's don't deliver to your front door.

The final part of the 148-year story comes just 9 months prior to the start of my race. The unique lighthouse optic, weighing 2 tonnes and worth around £1million, had been dismantled for restoration and stored in a warehouse in Ilfracombe. During a series of high-value burglaries, the optic was stolen, and so far, hasn't been recovered[5].

As well as having a lighthouse, Hartland Point also marks the western end of the Bristol Channel, the water magically turning into the Atlantic Ocean as it passed an invisible line stretching out to St Govan's Head in Pembrokeshire.

Just before passing the entrance to the lighthouse, a stone memorial on the left remembers the *Glenart Castle* sinking. The ship was around 20 miles out to sea from this location and clearly lit as a hospital ship, but in the early hours of the 26th of

---

[5] A bit of research 10 months after the theft shows no sign of it having been recovered. The chances are, it was quickly melted down and the valuable minerals sold on, a sad end to a piece of history.

February 1918 was hit by a torpedo from a German U-boat. With the lifeboats destroyed, the ship sank with the loss of 162 people including many of the ship's officers and medical staff.

Passing the lighthouse, the path turned to the right and we start heading in the 'right' direction – east. Continuing along tracks running across undulating grassy areas, there were occasional glimpses along the coast towards Westward Ho! and Morte Point.

In the more immediate foreground was a large white ball perched atop a concrete stick, looking like a massive and slightly odd-shaped mushroom.

Originally part of RAF Hartland Point, the mushroom is West Titchbury Radar station. Beginning life in 1941 as a VHF intercept station working as part of the Enigma code breaking operation at Bletchley Park, it later became a Chain Home Low radar station. The original radar system – Chain Home – could detect aircraft approaching, but would lose sight below around 5,000ft, but the new Chain Home Low system fixed this issue. Having a narrow beam, it used rotating radar heads and could detect aircraft down to around 500ft at a distance of 25 miles.

When I started writing these books, I'd never heard of "Chain Home", but it turns out you can't go much more than a mile or two on the South West Coast Path without bumping into something related to war-time radar installations. If that sort of thing floats your boat, it's worth digging into it. A lot of the foundational work for radar – and early telecommunications a good 40 or 50 years prior – happened in various coastal places between Poole and Minehead.

Just before the radar tower, there were some steps down to Hartland Point car park. As I was heading down the steps, clacking my way along with my poles, I passed a guy walking the other way carrying nets and various other nautical stuff. I said a jovial "morning!", to which he just replied with a grunt. People who do real, physical jobs probably look at us lot running past with our shiny race numbers and walking poles, thinking we should be doing something bloody useful instead of getting in the way, pointlessly running from one place to another!

Along from the car park, the path headed right along the coast beside the radar tower. There was a faint humming coming from under the white top, which up close looked a lot like some kind of taught fabric, roughly approximating a sphere. It was also surprisingly big – as always seems to be the case, things are a lot bigger when you're really close. Funny, that.

A little over a mile later, I was running slowly and easily along a corridor of path with large bushes either side. I heard voices just ahead, and as I caught up with two chaps running along, I could hear they were talking about the Arc of Attrition… so, obviously, I joined in, and we all got chatting.

I stuck with Matt Dalton and Andy Mutter for the next few miles, and we chatted about all sorts of things. Matt was doing 12 one-hundred mile runs in 12 months through 2022, raising money for Prostate Cancer UK, and this was his ninth of the year. He certainly wasn't picking easy ones either - he'd started with the Arc of Attrition in January and was now in the early stages of knocking out 110 miles along this tough stretch of coastline.

Matt seemed to know the organisers at Climb South West well, and I think this was his third time of doing the North

Coast event at one distance or another. Both he and Andy had also run the Jurassic Extreme 120 earlier in the year.

The chat was very interesting to me, as the Jurassic 120 was on my radar, having seen it on Facebook on that post-marathon Monday back in June, which then set me on the path to being right where I was today.

I came away thinking that these two were both sloggers, hard workers that got big ultras done in decent times. The discussion had got me thinking that the 120-mile event may be a bit of an ask for me... but then I've had that thought before and managed to complete long events. I decided it was probably a good idea to see what the next 36 hours brought, rather than worrying about the next event just yet!

During our chat, I noticed that the race had been going for just around an hour. As has been the case for several years now, my nutrition plan involved minimal carbohydrates on race day until an hour of running had passed, the idea being that raising the effort level without eating anything helps convince my body to make use of fat as the primary fuel source. After an hour or so, I can shove in as many carbs as I like without hugely affecting my ability to keep efficiently burning the fat, the carbs keeping my brain in a good, happy state, but not reducing the use of fat by my muscles. In that way, I could have about half the amount of carbohydrates I would have needed had I not done the prior preparation of a few months of low carb eating. Like I say, that's the *theory*, and it's probably all bollocks, but I just consider it part of my race routine, like some people have their lucky pair of pants.

I cracked open an Aldi Chocolate & Raspberry Vegan Flapjack. I'm not a vegan - far from it (several things have probably given that away, not least the steak last night) – but I liked the look of these on the shelf in the supermarket. The best thing about not being a vegan is that you can eat meat *and* vegan things! And actually, these flapjacks were really, really nice, going down easily, which isn't always the case for me with sweet things even just an hour into a race.

Matt and I had been chatting away and moved a little ahead of Andy, and as we were running along, winding around the edge of various fields, Matt mentioned that he thought there was a fort somewhere around here. He was right.

Windbury Hillfort sits 460 feet above the sea on the edge of Beckland Cliffs, and the site would have provided great protection from invaders for the settlers over 2,000 years ago. Earthen banks offered protection from inland approach, but most of these have been lost to sea erosion. The National Trust is working hard to preserve what is left, although, to the untrained eye of a couple of blokes running past on the coast path, there's not really a lot to see.

Very soon after passing the fort, we lost a good 350 of those 460 feet in a switchback descent into a valley, which we then immediately climbed straight back up the other side of.

Once I'd got my breath back, and as we carried on chatting about races, hill forts, views and towns, we again dropped down on another zigzag, this time all the way to sea level at Mouthmill Beach. We stepped our way across rocks in the water of the stream that ran out to sea, then turned inland to climb again up another 300-odd feet. The climbs weren't particularly memorable around here, I think partly because I was warmed up and finding them tolerable, and the conversation with Matt was making the time pass easily. Also, my focus was on getting to Clovelly so I'd start to see things that I remembered, and remember things that I'd forgotten from previous excursions.

I'd started with water in two half-litre soft-flasks, one on each side of my race vest. I had the spare in the back (the *new* spare, without the hole), but I figured that even though the first stretch was a little over 20 miles, I should be fine with 1 litre. In the past, I used to get through a litre in about 10 miles, but going at "ultra" pace, generally on cooler days, I seemed to be able to go 10-15 miles without any water at all, although doing so did have a tendency to catch up with me at that point and I tended to then get very thirsty all of a sudden.

The problem with today is that it was warm, really surprisingly so, and I was trying to meter out the water, to avoid drinking too much so I had it left for the latter stages. But I was actually feeling thirsty, and what I really wanted to do was drink quite a lot right now, despite having had a good litre or so on the bus this morning.

The route entered some fairly dense woodland with tall trees, green foliage, and roots to avoid tripping over. The path wound along for a while, then passed an unusual stone seat with a roof held up by what looked like angel's wings.

Built in 1826, the structure – unsurprisingly called Angel's Wings – was carved by a former butler of Clovelly Court for Sir James Hamlyn-Williams, owner of the Clovelly estate. The location offered a beautiful view across Bideford Bay, and it was said that Hamlyn-Williams would sit and look across the expanse to Youlston, where his daughter, Lady Chichester, had lived. After falling into a state of disrepair during the early 20th century, the structure was restored in 1934 by Boon Bros, boatbuilders of Northam which, incidentally, was where checkpoint 1 was located and where I was heading right now.

Matt was running well, and because of the water situation, I was holding back a little. We must have parted somewhere a little before here because I don't remember how, but I do remember that I was on my own for this bit. There was some more winding through the woods, and then I went through a gate into the bottom corner of a large grassy area, which stirred up a whole bunch of mixed emotions.

7

In search of water

Friday, 09:57

The field I'd just entered was the point where, just over a year before, I'd had a fateful night in a tent on my attempt to walk the whole of the South West Coast Path. I'd covered 105 miles over 3 days of walking coming from Minehead, was exhausted and on this particular night I had almost no sleep.

I was with my friend Chris, and as we'd pitched tents in the dark, concentrating more on finding a flat spot than paying attention to what we were pitching under. I ended up spending 2 hours laying on an inflatable mat inside a tent, convinced I was going to be crushed by a falling branch from the tree that was creaking around above my head in the wind. A quick midnight exploration of the area around the tree had me finding concerning chunks of log which, in the beam of my head torch, looked like they had recently fallen. And that was how it came to be that a tired bloke ended up dragging his partially dismantled tent ten metres across the grass in a field just outside Clovelly one pitch black September night.

As I closed the gate behind me in the daylight, a few miles into today's race, I noticed exactly the same branches on the ground around the tree… and no more. So, nothing had fallen off over the last year. I guess some things can seem a bit more perilous in the middle of the night!

Here I was, with the memory of that poor night's sleep and the moment that significantly changed my South West Coast Path walk. But right now, racing the North Coast, the feeling was very different: I was excited! I was now on the start of the section I'd covered before and it felt a bit… homely, somehow more comforting, knowing that I'd already done this bit before. And in daylight, places have a very different feel to the night – the sun brings a much more uplifting vibe than the off-white, patchy light of a headtorch.

I knew all I had to do was go through this little area of grass, then I was at the top of Clovelly, the first real milestone of the race with pretty much exactly 100 miles left to go, not that I let myself think about that.

The grassy park area, however, was bigger than I remembered, so I took the opportunity to whip out my little timing chart and see how things were going as I approached the first entry on the list. The time on the chart for Clovelly was 9:56am, but I had to add on 26 minutes due to our late start, meaning my target time was 10:22am. A glance at my watch told me that right now, it was 10:06am. It would be another few minutes before I'd be at the top of the village, so that meant I was about 10 minutes ahead of time. Perfect. Not too slow, not too fast, I was happy with that.

As I approached the exit gate of the grassy area, a look behind showed someone running along a little way back. I wasn't 'racing' in any way right now – in fact, I'd enjoyed the chatting with Matt and thought it would be nice to start a conversation with someone else as well. As I was taking it easy, I figured they'd catch me up soon.

Through the gate I was back on woodland trail, which went on a lot further than I remembered. I was back on the section of coast path that I knew – or at least *thought* I knew – yet within the first half a mile or so I'd completely misremembered the distances! This didn't bode well, although it wasn't any great surprise to me, given my catastrophic sense of anything navigational.

Eventually, after running gently through another green grassy area which turned out to be the one I thought I was in earlier much closer to Clovelly, I reached a big wooden gate and saw Matt a little way ahead. There were lots of cars parked in a big off-road area in front of me, along with a noisy, putt-putting buggy with a trailer doing bin-management of some variety and blocking the way. I was pretty sure I knew where to go but given how easily I seemed to find getting lost, I thought it best to push a little here to make sure I kept Matt in sight.

It really was as simple as I thought though – across Mount Pleasant, which is the area at the top of Clovelly – and ahead to a large wooden and metal gate signed "Hobby Drive". Hanging from the gate was another sign warning "Shoot in Progress". Probably best not look like a pheasant then!

Hobby Drive, or *The Hobby* was constructed between 1811 and 1829 as a scenic carriage drive by the previously mentioned Sir James Hamlyn-Williams. The Industrial Revolution had increased the emphasis placed on science and logic, and the Hobby Drive was born of the Romantic movement which celebrated beauty in the natural world. Over its two-and-a-half-mile length it offers breath-taking vistas high above the Atlantic, and today there are fine examples of internationally important lichen. To me, it's one of several places along the coast path that bring to mind a rainforest, full of green life, with a lingering dampness in the air.

As it was designed to survive the battering afforded by horses' hooves and metal-bound carriage wheels, the stony surface of the Hobby is quite hard. There was a spread of thin vegetation and dirt along the top in patches, but underneath it seemed to be composed of little pebble-shaped stones rigidly set into the ground that served to poke through shoe soles and push on the bottom of feet. Just a little bit, mind… not enough to be painful, just an annoyance, at least initially.

Around the entrance to the drive, the figure I'd seen behind me minutes earlier caught up and turned out to be Andy. He and Matt ran on slowly while I opted for a fast walk as the first section was slightly uphill, and a little way ahead, they switched back from running to walking.

Now, I have a decent walking pace – it's something I practice specifically for ultramarathons, as I figure I'm going to be doing a lot of walking, so I might as well try and get both faster and more efficient at it. It wasn't long before I caught up with Matt and Andy and sailed past to shouts of "Look at him go!" and "We've got a speedy one here!".

"You'll catch up with me in a minute," I said, fully meaning it, as I had intended to walk this section, or at most only do a little bit of very slow running. And sure enough, when the terrain flattened and started descending a little, they passed me by again.

Although a flat, wide track, the drive is definitely undulating. I was thinking about the terms to describe it while walking along – is "flat" the right term? I think so – the undulations were on a scale of a few hundred metres generally, so you'd have maybe quarter of a mile of gentle uphill, then a level section, then quarter of a mile of downhill. There was nothing technical about it – no roots to trip over, no cracks or particularly jutting rocks.

But there were those annoying pebble-like stones that made the whole surface an irritatingly tactile affair, constantly digging into the soles of my feet a little with every step and beginning to bring on the foot equivalent of a toothache. Maybe it was because I remembered how annoyed I got at the terrain on the walk a year ago that set me up for the expectation, but I was not even half way through and really beginning to hate this bloody drive!

I'd swapped places with Matt and Andy a few times over the various sections, but running is much quicker than even my fast walking and they'd started to gain a bit of a lead now, heading off into the distance as the drive wound its way along the contours of the land.

Every so often there was a sharp corner, an almost 180-degree about-turn usually over a little bridge that took me back on the other side of a stream running down the small valleys. All about were trees, ferns and moss, greens and browns spreading out as far as the eye could see. Occasionally, breaks in the trees gave views back to Clovelly harbour, or across Bideford Bay, but generally the route was undercover with a sense of being high up, the distant gentle noise of the sea making its way through the trees.

Taking advantage of walking rather than running, I had the remainder of my vegan flapjack, pleased with myself that I'd eaten a whole flapjack in an hour and wasn't feeling sick. That was better than my recent efforts, although still pretty poor considering I'd probably already burnt the best part of 1,000 calories and the flapjack had provided less than 200 of them as replacement. It would have been impossible to replenish everything I burnt in the race through eating, but I wanted to make a bit more of an effort than that.

Last year when I walked along the Hobby, after almost every corner I was met by a bunch of pheasants who did the usual thing of immediately dropping into an immense panic, flapping their wings a lot and running around, generally not going anywhere for quite a long time. But this year, I saw none. Given the sign on the gate at the entrance, I did wonder if, maybe, they'd all been picked off by shotgun wielding pheasant-hunters. It doesn't seem like much of a sport though, you'd have to try quite hard to miss one of them, given their haphazard way of trying to escape.

A couple of miles in, and the stones pushing on my feet really were starting to become a nuisance. No longer just an annoyance, the constant gentle bashing through my too-thin soles was starting to make the more prominent bones at the front of my feet hurt quite a bit. I wasn't too concerned – after all, what could I do about it? – but I just really, really wanted it over with.

It was hot, too. And humid. I was sweating a fair amount, regularly taking my cap off, shaking off a load of soaked up sweat, and wiping my brow. I sipped away at my water bottles, but kept trying to hold back on drinking as I judged I was only about half way to checkpoint 1.

There was a potential water refill opportunity in a mile or so though. Knowing this was the biggest single segment of the race – the start to checkpoint 1 being around 22 miles – and also remembering that last time I was here I had issues finding water, I'd done some research beforehand. While looking at the maps, I didn't spot anything obvious, but when Eva also had a look at the route, she quickly found a campsite just off the path. A Google of the site found it had a little shop, and although it was out of season in early October, it may still be open if there were people camping over the weekend. Failing that, most campsites have water taps that should still be working. On the map it looked to be only a short detour from the path, not far at all. But… there were many reasons why I might not be able to get water from there, so I'd been rationing what I had up to now, my thinking being that if I *did* find a tap, I could quench my thirst and leave with full bottles, so turning up a little dehydrated wouldn't matter. It would be better to save water and top up, than to drink it all early, not find anywhere and have to go a number of miles at the end of the stage with no water at all. I've made that mistake before, and it's very unpleasant.

Mercifully, those irritating pebbles on the ground eventually met a gate, the other side of which was beautiful soft grass! It felt so nice, like I'd just swapped super-hard shoes for the most cushioned one's imaginable.

On the grass, my joy at the nicer terrain had brought a spring to my step and I soon caught back up with Matt and Andy, although they must have been taking it easy as I certainly hadn't been going particularly fast.

I mentioned the turn for the campsite coming up and that I was going to go and get some water, suggesting maybe they'd want some as well? Neither seemed particularly interested, a testament either to their preparation or their lack of worrying about these sorts of essentially inconsequential things that seem to bother me so much on races.

I'd added a marker to my watch to show the camp site location so I zoomed out a little on the watch map to make the flag visible on the screen and I could see where it was in relation to my current position. I was a bit surprised – it was supposed to be just off the end of Hobby Drive, but I'd had to zoom out quite a long way to find the flag. Looking up from my watch, I was greeted with a grass field which, at our current pace, was going to take the best part of 5 minutes to cross.

It was beginning to dawn on me that my sense of scale when planning before the race might have been a bit off – that sense of scale you get when you're on a comfortable chair at the kitchen table, looking at a map and thinking "ahhh, it's only there, that'll be fine."

Turning into some trees at the far end of the grassy area, maybe 10 minutes after leaving the Hobby Drive, I finally found the narrow, muddy, overgrown path that was a right-turn off the coast path and headed to the camp site.

I said to Matt and Andy that I was turning off here and I'd hopefully catch them up, then banked right. I ran along the narrow path for maybe 30 seconds, then glanced at my watch. The flag marker had hardly moved. It was going to be a good 3 or 4 minutes to the end of the path. Then a few more minutes finding a tap, if I was lucky. Then 3 or 4 minutes back. That would be 10 minutes lost on a water hunt with what I judged to be less than a 50% chance of success.

"Fuck it," I said to a bunch of bushes, trees and maybe a squirrel, then turned around. I still had about 750ml of water, and it wasn't *that* hot. I must be over half way along this stage now, that really should be enough I told myself.

I think the desire to make up for the short amount of lost time meant I was unconsciously going a little faster than I intended to, as it wasn't long before I caught up with the other two again.

Since turning out of the grassy field a little before that campsite turn, the route had been under tree cover on dirt tracks with a plenty of tree roots to avoid tripping over. We crossed over a wider track heading perpendicular to us, and at the intersection was a finger post with distances to various places. I didn't even both looking at it.

The distance markers on the South West Coast Path can be somewhat… random. OK, the route changes fairly regularly as bits of the original path fall into the sea, or a grumpy landowner manages to re-route a right of way, but I can't quite understand how some of them can be *so* wrong. It always seems to be the newest ones that are the worst too, which rather buggers up the "re-routed path" argument I just suggested. I remembered from last year that the ones around Buck's Mills and Peppercombe, which I was now near, were particularly inaccurate, intermediate markers randomly having larger distances to any destination than the ones either side.

Hence my ignoring the marker. And also, because I knew roughly where I was, and that Buck's Mills couldn't be far away.

Coming the other way, I remember the hill out of Buck's Mills being never-ending – not particularly steep after the first section, but with so many false summits. Mind you, I was a good 25 miles into the walking day and getting pretty desperate for the end, which can change the perception of the terrain. Given that memory, I was looking out for a long continuous drop down to the village, but suddenly I was on a stone path, passing houses on the left, almost at the bottom of the hill. Last year, I'd had a chat with a chap in one of the houses who'd gifted me a dead fly, but this year no-one was outside as we headed down the final section of path to the main street through the village.

We took a right turn, not wanting to go sight-seeing on the coast today, and Matt yelled out to someone parked up on the right-hand side of the road. Matt's one of those people who seems to know everyone, which on this occasion was really handy.

"Have you got any water for Rich?" he shouted.

"Yeah, I've got loads," was the reply.

"Amazing, thank you!" I said, as I pulled out my most depleted soft flask, swigged as much as I could out of it quickly, and unscrewed the lid.

"It's just out the fridge," said the chap, who's name I never got, as he poured really cold water into my bottle. I thanked him again, probably more than once, as I was genuinely really grateful. This would see me through to checkpoint 1 no problem, and for someone who gets a little hung up on worries like this, it was a really big deal.

Matt and Andy had started up the steps at the beginning of the hill to the east of Buck's Mills. I had a good swig of the delicious cold water from the soft flask as I headed up in their direction, then spent far too long arsing about trying to get my partly drunk floppy soft flask back into my vest, whilst simultaneously concentrating on not tripping over on the uneven ascent out of the village. I eventually got my flask ensconced in its vest pocket, and then took stock.

Despite the relief from now having a decent amount of water, I was still had a niggling feeling that things didn't feel quite right.

8

Unexpectedly knackered

Friday, 11:09

Climbing a hill was always going to feel harder than not climbing a hill, but my legs were feeling a lot heavier than they really should do this early into a race. Overall, we hadn't covered that much distance or hit too many hills, just around 15 miles and a little over 3,000ft of climbing. And I certainly hadn't been pushing it pace wise. I resolved to make sure I didn't skimp on water and tried to eat more food, as those were 2 things that were under my control that could significantly affect how I was feeling. With that, I liberated Lidl's version of a Peperami from my vest and chomped it down. Not as good as a real one, but still quite nice if you like spicy, processed, fatty, meaty things. But whatever it tasted like, it was calories, fat, protein and salt – all stuff that should help.

The hill didn't get any harder, and although it took a few minutes, I was soon at the top. Given my heavy legs, Matt and Andy were far more capable than me on the ascents and had put in a fair amount of distance by the time I crested the summit of Mount Buck's Mills. As I continued on the woodland path through Worthygate Wood, I only caught the odd glimpse of them in the distance over the next few minutes before losing sight altogether.

I passed another coast path marker post which I duly ignored, knowing that Peppercombe was the next significant stop in a mile or two, and that the distance on the sign would be wrong anyway.

As Worthygate Wood silently turned into Sloo Wood, occasional breaks in the trees granted impressive views across the bay towards Westward Ho!. I remembered the terrain past Peppercombe being much more open, mainly fields and hedge-bordered paths over what looked like gently undulated ground, but I also knew it was a bit deceptive as the view extended a long way, making the hills look smaller than they actually were.

The cliffs on the seaward side weren't the classic bare chalk or sandstone that I was used to on the Jurassic Coast, but more gradual descents that allowed vegetation to grow, giving it a much greener look on the slopes down to the beaches. Where the rocks were exposed, they had a deep red colour, an outlier rock type that extends about 2km inland, a pocket that survived the erosion of the new red sandstone that used to cover a much larger part of Devon.

The best view was at the top of the descent down to Peppercombe, and that view soon disappeared as the path wound through dense woodland, popping out onto a track wide enough for cars. To the left, the beach and some interesting waterfalls where the stream that forms Peppercombe[6] meets the sea. The coast path, however, headed

---

[6] *Combe* comes from the Welsh word "cwm" which means "valley", and there are loads of place names containing combe all over this area.

right, past Peppercombe Coach House – a building that offers shelter and nothing more (said as someone who was desperately looking for water last time I passed and found none in here!).

This level road at the bottom of the hill by the Coach House was the second point on my timing chart, so I dug around in the front of my vest and extracted the sticky-tape covered bit of paper. Adjusting for the late start, I was due here at 11:58am. The time now was 11:40am; despite my heavy legs, I was just under 20 minutes ahead of my target time.

A turn to the left took me back onto the coast past, and I had a moment of mental boost, thinking it wasn't too far now to Westward Ho!. I'd remembered correctly that the terrain opened out here, although I could only see a few hills into the distance so there was no view of the promised town. The sky was much more visible without tree cover, and although there was some haze and the sun wasn't exactly beating down, the warmth seemed to step up a notch.

There was a little over 5 miles to go to the first checkpoint, and those miles had a certain up-and-down-ness about them. There were flat sections, and the hills weren't huge, but they weren't tiny either. As the climbs came one after another, they took their toll. I wasn't quite 17 miles into this 110-mile race. And, honestly, I was feeling shit.

I've done quite a few ultramarathons, and there have been many points early on where I didn't feel that great. It's always a bit worrying, but experience has shown that it never really amounts to much. I've always put it down to an expectation difference – I think that it *should* feel easy for the first 10 or 20 miles of a really long run, but in reality, it never does. But by the time I get to 40 or 50 miles in, I expect to feel a bit knackered, so the expectation matches the reality, and I that helps my mental state.

But today, something was different. On every uphill, my legs felt like lead. Breathing was fine, effort level wasn't high, but climbing was like someone had switched the muscles off in my legs. This was unusual, it was way too early in a race this long – especially at the relatively minimal effort level – to be feeling like this.

Half way up a fairly considerable hill, as all the energy had drained from my legs and I was plodding up step-by-slow-step, I passed another guy stopped by a bench. I figured he was doing his shoe laces up or adjusting his bag or something, but as I passed, I saw he was just looking out, and a brief exchange of words suggested he was just pausing for a break. It really wasn't that big a hill, and although I wasn't feeling great, I was surprised that another runner was stopping half way up.

I passed him by and continued on up the hill, and a little further along he caught up with me. Running at a similar pace, the silence became a bit awkward, so we started chatting and it quickly became apparent that he felt similar to me – unusually knackered for this early in a race. We dissected the situation, both a bit confused by how we felt, and the only thing we could think of was that it was a lot hotter than we'd expected and we weren't drinking enough. I was thinking about how I'd almost finished my two bottles, having topped one of them up, making it significantly over 1 litre that I'd drank so far. I was back to trying to ration water as there was still 4 or 5 miles left to do – somewhere around an hour on this terrain – which can feel like a very long time if you've run out of water and are thirsty. If this was the way the day was going to go, I needed to make sure I was better equipped, although I knew that this was a particularly barren section, and the others should have more frequent top-up opportunities.

I hadn't eaten anything for a while, so I opened an SiS chocolate fudge flapjack, something I quite enjoy on moderate length runs. The taste was alright today, but my dry mouth was making it difficult to chew and swallow, and a bit foolishly I didn't want to use up water by needing more of it because I was eating. So, I tucked the remainder of the flapjack away.

Unusually for me, I seemed to be dropping back on the flatter and downhill sections, so I was on my own again as I descended the path down to the beach. I'd been waiting for this bit – I remembered a section where you went all the way down a fairly significant hill to the beach, only to walk a few steps across some pebbles, go up some wooden steps and then you were back climbing again to the same level you were when you started the descent the other side. Typical coast path! What with it being on a bloody coast and all that…

So, I did just that. At the bottom of the steps, I skittered along a rocky section of beach, paying absolutely no attention to the coastline, the views or anything else other than the signpost signifying the start of the ascent back to the top of the cliffs.

As I began to climb, the energy in my legs quickly evaporated and I was back to the death-march up to the top, at which point I caught back up with Chris. I didn't know his name at the time, but I ended up spending a fair chunk of time with him over the next 12 hours.

We weren't far from Westward Ho! now, at least that's what I thought when the hedges parted and the narrow path widened to a flat, well-kept loose gravelly track, big enough to drive a car along.

With it being flat and less than 20 miles into a long ultramarathon, I really should have been running. But it was genuinely unpleasant each time I tried, so I ended up mostly trying to power along at a decent walking pace.

Chris and I silently exchanged places along this track that turned out to be far longer than I remembered. There wasn't any chatter as we both worked on keeping moving along, silently wondering why we both felt as shit as we did.

Then the path curved around to the right, a big moment. The approach to the town, with all its holiday parks and other nonsense, and just beyond, the first checkpoint.

First, some caravans. Then some more caravans. Then a few more – not completely unexpected for a caravan park. Then out onto the wide promenade, the Westward Ho! sea pool carved from the rocks on the left, looking a lot more like a pool than I remembered from last time. On the right, the words embossed on the ground in a mosaic started coming to me… "esiw oot klat ron…" It wasn't making a whole lot of sense backwards, so I went back to concentrating on making forward progress, occasionally glancing over to see if I could remember the source of the words. If you're wondering, it's the poem "If" by Rudyard Kipling.

When running is hard work, and you're struggling to make progress, there's little point doing it alone when someone else in the same situation is a few metres away, so Chris and I ran together along this final stretch to checkpoint 1. We were both discussing how the running felt horrible, but also that it would get us there sooner so it was a better option than walking.

One thing I was thinking is how much less of a dive Westward Ho! was than I remembered from last year. Back then, I was most unimpressed with the place – full of rude tourists, loud amusement arcades and with just a generally grotty feel. But today, it seemed much nicer. The walls of the buildings were bright white, there weren't as many amusement arcades as I thought, and there were far fewer irritating people about. Well, there were far fewer people about, which immediately increases the quality of a place for me.

Chris was from Bideford, I learnt. Which was handy as, being only a few miles further down the road meant he knew this area well. Which, in turn, meant I didn't have to bother with any of that navigation nonsense as long as I kept him in sight.

As we turned left and headed up a path towards some colourful beach huts, I pointed out to Chris that this wasn't the route that I had on my watch.

"Oh, it's OK, I know this way, the checkpoint's just over there," said Chris.

This is always a bit awkward. I was now a fair way along a route that wasn't technically correct. But to turn around and head the "right" route would not only add a bit of distance but could also come across as a bit rude. I quickly zoomed out on my watch map and determine that although the other route went along the front of a few buildings, there wasn't actually a significant difference in distance, so I just carried on following Chris past some beach huts.

We came to an interesting "pebble chicane" laid out on the path in front of us, with a winding pebble-free track through the middle.

Initially, I thought this was quite cute, a way to make a boring concrete path a bit more scenic and interesting. But when a couple of big families with dogs were making their way at a very leisurely pace towards us along the narrow path, it became a bit more annoying. What has looked like a pretty bit of pavement furniture had become a bloody nuisance, both Chris and I having to make our way along a load of slippery, wobbling pebbles as there was no room on the path. No problem on a quick training run, but over 20 miles into an ultramarathon and feeling every one of those miles in my legs, it was unappreciated.

All good things must come to an end. The same goes for all annoying things, and it really was only seconds before I was back on level ground in the corner of a dirt car park on the edge of Northam Burrows. Ahead, blowing in the wind like a paper bag, was a gazebo, and next to that, a flapping Climb South West flag.

It may only have been four poles and a canvas roof, but it was a very welcome sight after 22 tougher-than-they-should-have-been miles!

Checkpoint 1 – Northam Burrows

Distance	**22.1 miles**
Elevation	**5,110ft**
Time	**13:00 – 13:04** (target: 13:10)
Elapsed Time	**5 hours 4 minutes**
Position	**10th**
Split Position	**10th**

110 Mile Competitors Remaining: **21**

It was time for a drink and some food. As I approached the gazebo, I pulled the two soft-flasks out from my vest, a technique I'd used to reduce time at aid-stations. Over the last few metres, I squeezed the contents of the fuller of the two flasks into my mouth, and began to unscrew the tops, ready to be refilled as soon as I arrived.

That makes it sound like I was going to dash in and dash out of the checkpoint, which, on a shorter ultra might have been the case. I hadn't mentioned to the part of my brain in charge of getting my bottles ready that today, though, I had absolutely no intention of rushing through. Some other, more sensible part of my brain had decided that I'd covered a fairly lumpy 22 miles, was feeling a bit shit and was going to have a bloody rest for a minute or two.

"This is the most people I've had here so far," said the bloke under the gazebo, rushing around tending to everyone's need. He really couldn't have been any more helpful – he was filling water bottles, offering tea, coffee and food, asking if there was anything else we needed and checking we were happy to go on. He filled both my flasks up to the brim, one with water and the other with orange squash.

Orange squash. Yep. Not Tailwind, or Torq, or any of that technical nonsense, but Tesco's own double-concentrated (or maybe quadruple-concentrated) squash. Almost certainly sugar-free as well.

A part of me was thinking that I'd paid the best part of two-hundred quid to do this race, maybe they could have supplied some "proper" sports nutrition, as it's the only time I ever get "proper" sports nutrition (I don't use it during training).

But then, I also loved the fact that… well… it was up to *us*. You want nutrition – carbs, protein and fat? Well, sort that out yourself (at least the liquid form). We'll supply you with hot drinks and water, sometimes flavoured, but the adventure – and the responsibility – is yours to make sure you've got what you need. After all, this is what they said in the info pack.

With that, I grabbed a packet of crisps and a couple of mini-sausage rolls. So yeah, there was plenty of edible snacks available - from sweets to crisps to savoury snack, some meaty and some vegan. Everything you might need to *top up*, which again, was exactly the point. It was refreshing, especially as this had been my approach coming into the race. If I'd expected to have my hand held through every checkpoint, I would have been disappointed.

9

Golf, rubbish and a little stretch of water

Friday, 13:04

You may think that being only 22 miles into a 110 mile race would be a bit daunting – after all, there's still just under 90 miles to go which is a fairly intimidating distance, longer than a lot of pretty long races.

But I don't think like that during ultramarathons, it genuinely very rarely crosses my mind to contemplate the whole thing now. My mind is solely focused on just the next segment, usually to the next checkpoint, but sometimes to key points along the way that I can mentally tick off. It's much more tolerable when you're thinking about the next 10, 15 or 20 miles – a few hours – rather than focusing on 100 miles in the future, maybe more than a day away.

Right now, at Northam Burrows, it felt like I'd just completed the event, rather than having so much left to do. But it was time to switch my head into gear for the next section, the journey to Barnstaple.

I pressed a few buttons on my watch to stop the current course and choose the next one which was to the next checkpoint, and it showed 17.12 miles to go, a bit less than the 19 miles I, for some reason, had been expecting. It's always nice to have these little moments of positive news, but I also fully expected to make the odd wrong turn and add some miles to the total, so 19 was probably more realistic.

This Northam-to-Barnstaple segment was a totally different kettle of fish to the route from the start in just about every way. Where the first section had hills and was mostly off-road, away from civilisation, this second section was almost entirely flat, a good chunk on pavement or cycle path, and ran through the towns of Appledore, Bideford, Instow, past Fremington and on to Barnstaple. For one thing, getting a drink on this section should be a whole lot easier if I started to run low!

Being flat has obvious upsides, but also presents some challenges. First off, you're using the same muscles again and again, so the overall impact of a good long stretch of flat terrain can be more damaging to specific muscles than off-road, undulating terrain, which spreads the impact over more groups.

And secondly, there really is no excuse not to run, which can present a mental problem. Especially, when you don't particularly want to be running.

Thanking the guy crewing checkpoint one, I headed north from the gazebo through the remainder of the car park and onto a road. A bit of fiddling with my vest and my poles at the checkpoint had meant Chris and Andy – who had been at the checkpoint when I'd arrived – were a little ahead of me, which also meant I didn't have to think about navigation, just follow the leaders.

A bit of jiggling about between road and grass to avoid cars passing, and soon we were heading around the edge of the Royal North Devon golf course which, having been founded in 1864, had the honour of being the oldest golf course in England.

Northam Burrows is common land that was given the designation of Site of Special Scientific Interest (SSSI) in 1998, and the golfers share the land with sheep, ponies, walkers and idiots running 110-mile races along the coast path.

The golf course takes up the western half of the northern end of the peninsula, and the coast path occupies a narrow, sandy rut between the edge of the greens and the beach below. As I passed one of the tee areas, a guy swung and whacked his ball, moments later getting loud congratulations from his mates on his excellent shot. What stood out to me was how *young* they all were! I thought golf was an old man's game, but here were a bunch of blokes in their mid-20's.

The path continued along past a few more greens until it widened out on a bumpy stretch of grassland, the beach and water of the Taw & Torridge Estuary to the left and the golf course hidden behind mounds of grassy ground to the right. The terrain was a mix of short grass and sandy trails, with a few rabbit holes peppering the ground, making me worry about broken ankles! It didn't last long though, soon I was back on a narrow bit of path, the beach immediately to my left, and the seventh green surprisingly close on my right.

In the first couple of days of January 2018, Storm Eleanor wreaked havoc, both in the UK and across into Europe. During the storm, a 15m chunk of land was ripped away just beyond where I was now, leaving this part of the golf course just metres from the water. At the time, it was thought that more of the land would be washed away with the coming high tides and forecast adverse weather, with the probable loss of the whole green within a month or so. Despite requests from the golf course owners, Natural England who managed the land said "the dunes and shingle ridge are naturally dynamic coastal features and subject to constant change." So, tough, really. They did concede to them building two new greens further from the coast, but only if they relinquished two current ones within 3 years. But from the looks of things as I was passing, it seemed the predicted devastation failed to materialise.

Last year, as I was coming around the headland of Northam Burrows, I remember it being windy and hot, and I was in a bad mood that I was having to pointlessly go around the top of a lump of land when I could have just cut across to the other side lower down, for a moment somewhat missing the point of a *coast* path.

It turns out there's quite a good reason why it's not a good idea to cut across the middle of the burrows, and it's not a great testament to humankind. In 1936, rubbish dumping began on the north-eastern end of the burrows and continued on for more than half a century. Sections of the burrows are now cordoned off for safety reasons and given the erosion by the weather on the seaward end, there's some concerns about the risk posed by the whole site to the wider area. Over the years, it's said that everything from cyanide used in steel works, asbestos from the local Yelland power station, engine oil, used syringes and out of date medicines from hospitals, gas canisters and the contents of septic tanks have all been dumped here, as well as general household rubbish. Photos online show sections of a white membrane that keeps the rubbish contained – and should be hidden deep underground – exposed against the eroded edge of the sand right on the estuary of the Taw and Torridge rivers. Scary stuff, a very ill-thought-out location for mindlessly dumping thousands of tons of rubbish.

I was blissfully unaware that I was running on a thin veneer of ground atop almost 6 decades of rubbish. In fact, I was focused on the race and generally pretty happy, mixing running and walking, swapping places with Andy as we headed along to the coastline, feeling a whole lot better than an hour or two before.

Just ahead, Chris had taken a 90-degree right turn and was heading across a green area, and I felt like I was beginning to catch him up. As I then also turned right into quite a strong wind blowing right at me, slowing me right down, I realised *why* I'd appeared to be catching them up.

This particular point on the course was quite significant too, but not for an immediately obvious reason. If you got a bit of string with a weight on the end and lobbed it with great strength and excellent aim just under 1 mile almost directly east, you'd get your string tangled with the tubular steel supports of Crow Point Lighthouse. The significance? Crow Point is almost the spot at which you turn north and start heading away from the Taw and Torridge estuary. You're probably still confused... well, ahead of me was 23-and-a-half miles of path, through Appledore, Bideford, Instow, Fremington, Barnstaple, Chivenor and around the edge of Braunton before getting to… Crow Point. So, I was about to embark on a 23-and-a-half-mile detour to a point that was almost throwing distance away from where I was now. That's the coast path for you!

I can't mention a lighthouse without banging on a little about the history, and the Crow Point Lighthouse is not like any other I've seen (but I'm far from an expert, I just quite like lighthouses). It was built in 1954, and designed from the start to be a standalone, unmanned structure, its purpose to guide vessels down the Taw and Torridge estuary. A whopping 5 metres tall, it's basically a few scaffolding poles on top of a pile of rocks with a light on top. It was originally powered by acetylene gas like a lot of old lighthouses but was electrified in 1984 and can be seen for 6 nautical miles. I'll be honest, I've never knowingly seen Crow Point Lighthouse, I think it's one of those things that disappears into the background until night-time, but I'm sure it's saved a few boats from getting stuck on mud or crashing into rocks.

Back to the race... I was running into the wind, dropping back a little from Andy as I slowed and watching Chris lead the way in the distance. I slogged it out towards the end of Northam Burrows, hoping the wind wouldn't be a big part of the next few miles.

The grass turned to a road literally built on top of rubbish as the route headed towards the east, and the wind subsided a little. I kept the slow running pace going and didn't really lose any ground on Andy or Chris through the rest of the Burrows. The road turned to the left across the little Appledore Bridge which allowed vehicle and pedestrian passage across a tidal river known as The Pill[7], then past a wooden toll booth that looked closed. I would have followed the road around to the right had I followed my natural instinct, but luckily, I was

---

[7] Pill comes from the Welsh *Pil* and refers to a small tidal creek or inlet. It's commonly used along the Bristol Channel and Severn Estuary.

following some more competent navigators, so I went the right way instead. I was thinking that the whole circumnavigation of Northam Burrows Country Park had been surprisingly rapid and uneventful.

And here we are again, back to my recurring theme through these books: that your expectation of how something is going to feel has a massive influence on how you *actually* feel when it happens. After the hot slog around Northam last year, I wasn't looking forward to it during the race, expecting it to be tough. But today, it passed by quickly and easily, with interesting views and people to follow.

I crossed the grassy stretch, Andy and Chris leading the way some distance ahead, then through a gate in a fence and I was on the sand and pebbles of the Skern, a sort of mud-flat area nestled between Northam and Appledore.

The coast path route offers 2 options here. When the tide is in, you head up onto the bank and walk on a path along the very back of the small bay area. But today, the tide was out, and we could make our way across the dry sand and rocks to the far side, only a few hundred metres away.

Up from the sand, I gently ran along a walkway, white steel railings to my left, speckled with rust as everything near the sea tends to be, and past the picturesque Appledore Lifeboat station with its long concrete jetty extended outwards and descending into the water.

Irsha Street is a narrow road which plays host to the coast path for a moment, running along the seafront, with quaint white, yellow and blue pastel houses to my right and the Taw estuary to my left, Crow Point and Braunton Burrows tantalisingly close across the water, and yet so far away on foot.

The view to the left was replaced by houses and I was on the beautiful little street that I remembered being a feature of Appledore last time I was here. The road was ridiculously narrow, certainly not wide enough for two cars, and the terraced cottages were all sorts of bright colours: red, green, terracotta, pale pink and blue. There was a gentle hum of activity on the street, a mix of tourists, tradesmen and homeowners, a lovely normal day feel to the place as I ran along the road in the surreal headspace of an ultramarathon.

The road continued along a little, past the Beaver Inn, and then widened out next to a car park. My sense of navigation seems to be primarily based on heading towards obvious things, so I turned towards the enticing entrance of the car park, a vague niggling memory of having been a bit puzzled and making a mistake here last year. Just before I went into the car park, I caught a glimpse of brass in the pavement above, and it all came back to me.

In this area from Westward Ho! through Appledore and on to Bideford, the coast path markers aren't the usual wooden finger posts, but instead are lovely brass footprints embedded in the pavement. I hopped up onto the pavement and followed the footprints along the outside length of the car park, finally turning onto the quay at Appledore.

Tawmutha ("Mouth of the Taw") was the 14th century name for the area now known as Appledore, which began life as a fishing village. During Tudor times, thanks to connections with the likes of Sir Walter Raleigh, it became one of the largest importers of tobacco in the country. Later, it prospered as a busy shipbuilding hub, the quay being built in the early 19th century, and then widened during World War II. The ships built here were much in demand during both wars, with the location being seen as an ideal place for testing top secret weapons and equipment.

Warships and weapons aside, I'd been thinking on my way to Appledore that if I saw an ice-cream van on the front which didn't have a queue, I'd stop and grab a Mr Whippy with a flake to munch while wandering along. Any calories are good calories during an ultramarathon, right?

10

"Are you all completely mad?!"

Friday, 13:55

Sadly, as I went along the front, there were only 2 ice-cream vans and both had big families waiting for what looked like sizeable orders, so I continued on. I do this a lot – have some great idea about stopping in a shop for some food or drink – but rarely do. I hate the thought of wasting time and when I get to wherever I've been imagining, I almost always talk myself out of actually stopping.

On the left, Instow sat on the other side of the Torridge. I'd only gone half a mile since the start of Appledore, but I was now running along a different river. Just above Appledore, the water splits – heading north, the Taw continues 45 miles on through Barnstaple, and south the Torridge runs through Bideford and on a circuitous 58 miles to Higher Clovelly, just south of the village I'd run past a few hours before.

Although Instow was only about 600 metres away as the crow flies (and crows probably did actually fly across that little stretch of water), the route I was taking would get me there in about 7 miles. Where's the fun in going the direct route when you can wind your way around the houses?

I'd come up with a bit of a plan for this flatter section of the route. For now, I'd try and average 14-minute mile pace with a mix of running and walking. As my watch beeped indicating the start of a new mile, I'd run for a bit at a comfortable 9- or 10-minute mile pace, and then stop and walk for a bit to conserve energy, swapping between running and walking as I closed off the mile to try and hit 14 minutes. Not only did it give me a strategy that should stop me over-exerting myself or being too relaxed, but it gave me something to concentrate on too, a bit of mental stimulation.

The clouds above had been throwing light rain drops at me for the last few minutes, in itself, not enough to bother doing anything about. However, I'd looked at the weather forecast for today, and paid particular attention to the band of heavy, squally showers that were due to hit this section of North Devon sometime in the early afternoon. And being pretty much exactly 2pm, I was thinking the incoming weather was imminent.

Knowing what was likely to be coming, I thought it best to stop and get myself better prepared. I spied a bus shelter just ahead, adjacent to the big, old shipyard, where I could spend a minute in the dry getting myself ready for some rain.

As I approached the bus shelter, I was a little confused as to why there were books on the seat, and a couple of boxes underneath, then read the sign saying this was no ordinary bus shelter – this was Appledore Library! I put down my poles, took off my race vest and put it on the seat between a crime novel and something that looked like erotic fiction, then extracted my rain jacket. As I was getting myself zipped up, Andy passed me – I'm not quite sure how he ended up behind me as I'd been following him earlier, but that's the nature of these events. People stop to adjust shoes or packs, have a pee or various other things and the order swaps around.

"You haven't got time to read a book, Rich!" shouted Andy as he strolled past, already zipped up in his coat.

"Oh, I don't know," I said, "I might stop for a little rest." That would have been nice…

I finished faffing with my coat but didn't bother putting on my waterproof shorts. I'd already taken a bit longer than I wanted to, still trying to keep to that 14-minutes-per-mile plan, so wanted to get moving again. I figured if the rain got really heavy, I could pop the shorts on quickly, so with race vest back on and poles back in my hand I started off back up the street.

The road continued along beside a tall old stone wall, in the middle a black gate with wrought iron lettering proclaiming "RICHMOND DOCK". Rounding a corner, a bunch of older chaps were having a very loud and jolly beer-fuelled conversation under the overhanging shelter of a building.

"It definitely looks like there's some event going on," said one of them to the group, nodding in my direction.

"There's 20 or so of us doing a race," I said back as I passed.

"Oh, how far?"

"Er… a hundred and ten miles"

"WHAT?! One hundred and… are you all completely mad?!"

"Almost certainly," I replied with a big smile on my face. I have no shame in saying that I love it when you tell people who don't know about these sorts of events how far you're going. I seem to spend my life surrounded by people who either run stupid distances, or are completely fed up with hearing about running stupid distances, so to meet the odd person who is freshly amazed by the concept – a distance they think twice about driving, let along doing on foot – it makes me grin!

The road continued on, getting surprisingly narrow in places, interesting old stone walls to one side or the other, sometimes both. I was happily mixing running and walking, managing to comfortably keep to my planned pace and make decent progress.

I passed some new looking industrial buildings, the whole area having a very marine feel to it, not unsurprising given Appledore's ship building heritage. Occasionally visible through the bushes at the southern end of the village was a huge building – now Harland & Wolff, but originally the Appledore Shipbuilding company – which at the time it was built was the largest covered dry dock in Europe.

Shortly after passing the massive building the road gently climbed and just ahead was a wooden finger-post next to a stile, nicely lining up with a sharp left turn on my watch map. Over the stile, I was now back onto trail, but only for a couple of minutes before popping out onto a narrow road directly in front of a massive Range Rover! Thankfully, it was slow moving, and I put my hands up in apology and stepped back, by which point they had come to a stop and were distinctly gesticulating through the windscreen to their left. It took me a moment to realise that, rather than being angry at me, they were directing me back onto the continuation of the coast path route through a gap in the wall on the other side of the road. I quickly crossed the road, put my hand up in thanks and headed back onto the trail.

By now, the rain was heavy enough that I was very happy to be in a coat. So many times, you stop and faff around putting a coat on, only for the threat of rain to pass without ever really tuning into anything. Then, having got hotter and sweatier unnecessarily, you have to undo it all again, wasting more time. But today, it was, without a shadow of a doubt, the right choice.

What wasn't the right choice, though, was not putting on my waterproof shorts. My coat was decent, a good, solid waterproof coat. As such, the rain was beading, gathering in big droplets, then running down and off the bottom of the coat.

All over my shorts.

Which were getting really quite wet now.

Enough was enough. I was back out towards the coast now and there wasn't a lot of cover, ahead one fairly pathetic tree which would provide minimal shelter but would have to do. Under the ineffective cover of the tree, I reached around and pulled out my "wet and cold weather" drybag from my pack, unclipped it and whipped out the shorts from the top. They're more like over-shorts, so all I had to do was get my feet in and pull them up. The first foot was relatively easy, but then I had to balance to get the second one in. The 25 miles already in my legs threatened to topple me over, but I just about managed to get my foot in without face-planting on the cost path. With the outer, waterproof shorts on, I was happy. The shorts underneath were a bit wet but not soaking, and the warmth of running and walking would dry them out soon, there shouldn't be any risk of the wet fabric creating any hot spots or chafing.

And with the outer shorts on, barring a sustained torrential downpour, I should stay pretty dry.

Round the next corner, about 30 metres on from where I'd stopped, was a set of dense bushes, the ground underneath completely dry – the perfect point to shelter out of the rain. Bloody typical.

For a while, the path was a mix of woodland trail, boardwalks, firm sand sections, and narrow passages between fences and walls. It was mildly undulating, certainly not hilly but not flat either, just like your average walk in the woods. I tried to make the most of the mild hills, enjoying the way my legs worked in slightly different ways to being on the flat, knowing after these it would be pancake flat for a lot of miles.

The woods became sparser, and I hit a patch of muddy sand in the shadow of the new Torridge bridge. The trail split here – one low tide route across the sand, and another up a dark path which I opted for, having ended up with my feet sinking into the mud last year. The higher trail literally went just around the back of the sand, and 30 seconds later I popped out on a path that went across the front of a few nice-looking houses with their fronts facing out onto the river.

Ahead, a car was parked at the side of the road and a runner was changing shoes. As I passed, I realised it was Chris, and shouted out a hello. We'd been chatting while running into checkpoint 1 earlier, and he'd mentioned that he had crew and was going to change into road shoes at Bideford for the "flat bit".

Next was a small estate of new-ish brown houses, the coast path route following the road round a couple of corners and past a roundabout onto a footpath, at the end of which I could see the big car park on the end of Bideford Quay.

For the last few miles, I'd been enjoying the freedom of drinking whenever I liked, knowing – or at least *hoping* – that it would be far easier to top up along this stretch so making up for the lack of water in the first section. I'm not normally a fan of orange squash, but I'm also not picky so I'll have whatever is on offer at the aid stations. However, on this day, I'm not sure if it was because it was super strong or it was just one that I hadn't had before, but this orange squash was absolutely delicious. It tasted almost like fresh orange juice. And that had got me thinking about a drink at Bideford. I was pretty sure the squash was sugar-free, and the thought of a carton of fresh orange juice unusually appealed to me. Normally, I avoid it like the plague – 100g of sugar in a litre of drink is bordering on insanity for everyday drinking! – but today, it seemed like a delicious way to get some carbohydrates in.

I'd passed through Bideford last year and not gone into any shops (Wetherspoon's doesn't count, does it?), but it was a town, and towns have shops, so it couldn't be that difficult to find somewhere that sold some orange juice and a bottle of water. I'd really set my heart on that orange juice.

Running alongside the car park, which, in typical fashion, went on a bit longer than I remembered, I was enjoying the variety of boats on the water. I'm not sure any of them actually moved, in fact one of them may have been a café, but they looked like proper boats, all rusty metal, circular holes and huge ropes.

The path turned into the pavement of the A386, which was a little bit of a shock to the senses after almost 7 hours of mostly quiet paths. But I didn't care about that, I was on a mission.

As soon as I got on the quay front, I turned off course and crossed the main road, much to annoyance of my Garmin. I looked up the first road I came to – Bridgeland Street – but the only shop I could make out at the far end was Oxfam, and I didn't think they'd have orange juice.

Rather than waste a load of time wandering around aimlessly, I unzipped my vest pocket and got my phone out so I could look up where the nearest Tesco Express or Co-op was.

Touchscreens are brilliant. Add them to a phone, and you've got the perfect combination of flexibility and ease of use. Unless said touchscreen phone has been in a sweaty pocket for a few hours. The phone turned on when I pressed the side button, but the Face ID thingy flatly refused to recognise my face[8], and the touch bit of the touchscreen just totally ignored my fingers, so I couldn't type in the code to unlock it.

Another thing that's brilliant are technical fibres – you can make running stuff out of them, and they wick sweat away from the body, keeping you cool and dry (to some extent at least). But what they're really, really rubbish at is wiping touchscreens.

I poked the phone a while longer, occasionally wiping it against my shorts or t-shirt which just seemed to spread the sweat around. The best I managed was a few digits of my passcode with about 50 pokes of the screen, this was bloody

---

[8] I've since found that Face ID doesn't work if you've got slightly steamed up glasses on. Take them off, and it seems to work fine.

infuriating! What I needed was a tissue. Where was I going to get one of those?

I looked up the road at the shops, and as my eyes drew back from the Oxfam at the far end, they landed on The Rose Salterne.

The Wetherspoons Pub.

Right.

I'll go in, top up my water bottles as I happened to know from a previous visit that there was a water refill thingy at the back. While I'm doing that, I'll find a tissue – there's bound to be a dispenser somewhere – wipe my phone and find a Tesco's. Yeah, that'll work.

11

Choo Choo

Friday, 14:45

I got a couple of odd looks as I walked into Wetherspoons, a little wet, with poles and a race vest on my back. I went straight to the back, where I knew the water-thing was, and quickly filled up both my bottles with ice-cold water.

I looked around for some tissues to wipe my phone screen, but the only thing I found was a dirty, scrunched napkin on a plate of eaten food by the kitchen hatch. I thought about nicking it – mid-ultra, anything goes – but decided I'd ask at the bar.

So, there I was, standing at the bar…

The barman came over, and I asked if he had a napkin so I could wipe my phone screen. He fiddled around in his pockets and came out with a tissue… hmmm… I didn't think about *what* I was wiping my phone with, I just wiped it and, hey presto, it all worked again!

Have you heard the one about the bloke in the middle of an ultramarathon, standing at the bar with a phone that was now working…?

"Go on then… a pint of Doom Bar, please."

I explained a little about what I was up to while the guy was pouring my pint.

"You should have had a Guinness!" he said.

He handed me my pint and wandered off to do some more bartending. When he returned about 30 seconds later, I handed the empty glass back and thanked him.

"Blimey, you really did need that, didn't you," came the reply. "Good luck!"

I thanked him again as I walked through the pub, what I'd just done beginning to sink in. I couldn't undo it, but I was hoping I hadn't just made a huge mistake.

I've never, ever stopped for a beer in the middle of a race. I've often joked about it, but never actually done it. What happens now? It was one pint… I was hardly likely to fall over pissed as a fart outside, but would I still be able to run? Would I be clumsier, more at risk of twisting my ankle or something like that? Would my guts go mad?

At just after a quarter to three, an impressively quick four minutes after entering the fine establishment that is the Rose Salterne, I was heading out the door, down to the main road and back across the busy street, already being slightly riskier with the traffic than I would normally have been. I was beginning to feel… good!

I ran along the final stretch of the main road, passing a statue of Tarka the Otter, inscribed with thanks to the local councils and businesses and a quote from the book about the Bideford "ancient Long Bridge".

At 207m long, Bideford Long Bridge was one of the longest medieval bridges in England, and until the very late 18th century was the longest in Devon. It's 24 uneven arches – an artefact of the widths being dictated by the length of the timbers used for its original construction back in the 13th century – connects the formally important river port of

Bideford with the oddly (and aptly) named East-of-the-Water. It was rebuilt in stone in the 14th century, using the original wooden structure as supports, so the arches were forever set to be uneven. Back in them-there medieval times, you only needed to get a couple of horses across, so the bridge was quite narrow. In 1865, it was widened to accommodate more modern traffic, at one point even having a railway track laid along the top of the structure. Widened again in 1925, it became big enough to carry a couple of lanes of traffic with a pavement either side, which is how it stands today.

As I crossed over the centuries old Grade I structure, with all its ancient history hidden beneath a bog-standard tarmac roadway, the beer was bringing in a nice sense of relaxation, sweeping away worrying thoughts. Although it was early days, I had been concerned that I'd feel bloated and sick, but there was none of that. It just felt really nice!

At the far side of the bridge was a small roundabout, and I had a couple of roads to cross before heading up the steps that I could see opposite. It was nice to know where I was heading, I could just concentrate on getting there, rather than continuously looking at my watch or worrying about whether I was going the wrong way. I nipped across the first road through an opportune gap in the traffic, then someone in a Range Rover stopped to let me cross the other road. I'm not a fan of Range Rovers, but in the last hour, two of them had been nice to me, which was messing with my preconceived notion of what a Range Rover driver was like! I thanked them with a big thumbs up and a smile.

Chances are, if you're reading this book, you're probably a runner yourself. But if not, then if you're ever driving along a road and you see a runner trying to cross, do be nice and let them across (assuming it's safe and all that stuff). It's much appreciated when people in cars stop for you, especially in ultras; stopping and starting again can be hard work after a good number of miles and can break any rhythm you have.

I went up the steps, covered in those classic brown tiles that I remembered seeing on the footbridges of railway stations back in the 1980s, which wasn't too surprising as I was heading up to what would have, up until 1982, been Bideford Station.

Opened in 1855, the station was originally the terminus of the line from Barnstaple, but an extension in 1872 took it on to Torrington. As is the case with a huge amount of British railway stations, following Richard Beeching's report, the station closed to regular passenger services in 1965, and all rail traffic ceased in the early 80's.

After the closure of the line, a preservation society re-laid 200 metres of track and they occasionally run locomotives along it. As I reached the top of the steps, there were a couple of railway carriages and the old stone station building that together form the Bideford Railway Heritage Centre.

There's also a tarmac trail – the Tarka Trail – stretching off into the distance along the route of what would have been the railway track.

And, indeed, just over 10 years before, it was once again a railway track running all the way to Barnstaple. Had you wanted to travel on it, though, you'd have to have been less than an inch tall, as it was one of the challenges on James May's *Toy Stories* television program. They originally tried in 2009 to build a model railway between the two towns along the path of the original train line but failed due to vandalism and technical issues. Two years later[9], they tried again and successfully had a British team run model trains from Barnstaple to Bideford, and a German team in the other direction. That's one hell of a trip for a model train!

The Tarka Trail, named after the otter that fictionally frequented this neighbourhood, is 180 miles long and shaped vaguely like a figure of 8. The bit that I'd be going on overlapped with the South West Coast Path and headed to Barnstaple, then on to Woolacombe, Ilfracombe and Lynmouth, but the whole route itself heads south down as far as Okehampton on the northern edge of Dartmoor.

The first thing I passed was the back of the Royal Hotel, which was all white and clean at the front, but looked a bit of a mess from the back, at least to my eye as it vaguely skimmed in that direction. I then went under a bridge that carries Barnstaple Street, and that was about the last interesting thing that stuck in my mind for a while.

You see, this bit of the Tarka Trail is a flat tarmac cycle path pretending to be a railway line running for about 9 miles to Barnstaple, and there wasn't a huge amount to look at. Or at least, that's what I told myself, as I put my brain in a sort-of dormant mode, tasked with moving my feet along at a decent clip and not much else.

It occurred to me that I wasn't going to be needing my poles for a while, so I folded them up, thankful that the buttons holding them erect (don't be childish!) were still working OK. My favourite Leki poles were about 6 years old now, and recently the lock mechanism had started to fail. On inspection, I found the years of sweat and muck had built up around the

---

[9] "The Great Train Race", aired originally on 12th June 2011.

button that locks the sections together, so I gave them a thorough clean and oil and they worked nicely after that – and thankfully still seemed to be working reliably. With the poles folded down, I slipped them into the back of my pulse belt without breaking stride.

For most of the morning, I'd had Hans Zimmer's *No Time to Die* soundtrack going around in my head, having been listening to it a lot recently while at work. But on the path, under the influence of a small amount of beer, I was feeling good, and wanted to share my joy with the world. I started singing, and I offer my sincerest and most heartfelt apologies to anyone who heard my not-so-dulcet tones.

I had my watch set to lap every mile, at which point it offers a little beep to tell me I'd covered another 1,609,344 millimetres, and I was using that as a trigger to do some running. I would then run the first half-mile or so, maybe a little more, after which I'd drop back to a fast walk for the rest, averaging around 12-minute miles while gradually increasing the volume on my heavy-metal/jazz cross rendition of Dire Strait's *Sultan's of Swing*.

A long, pretty straight cycle path attracts a few things, one of them being bikes. They came nipping by occasionally, but much more politely than I'd remembered from the year before. Unsurprisingly, it seems mid-afternoon is a better time to wander along a cycle path than mid-morning commute-o'clock, as it had been for me last time I was on this trail.

The straightness also offers views of runners ahead, and on the occasional glance back, behind as well. Which brings that race element in… can I catch the guy in front? Will I be caught by the guy behind? (I'm not being sexist incidentally; I could see they were both blokes).

I'm probably going to make my earlier comment about there not being "a huge amount to look at" seem totally wrong now, as I run through all the things to look at between Bideford and Barnstaple...

Almost exactly a mile after joining at Bideford, there's the new and quite large Torridge Bridge, and this was my third contact with the thing so far today, the first being when I travelled along the top in a minibus about 9 hours before, and the second on the other side of the river, passing Chris as he was changing shoes in the back of a car.

Until 1987, the medieval Bideford Long Bridge that I'd crossed a mile or so before was the closest to the estuary, but then, 24 metres in the air, came the winner of the 1988 Concrete Society Award. At 650 metres long, it's quite an impressive lump of concrete to be fair. Although it was somewhat infamous for the wrong reasons, as originally it was pretty easy to jump off, so a surprising number of people did. Many people believe it was knocked down because of the number of suicides, but as I was passing underneath it again, I can attest to the fact that it's definitely still there. Either that, or it's a very persistent feature of my imagination.

I carried on singing, now on to some oddly twangy version of *Sweet Child O' Mine*, as the seemingly unending path continued on and on. At times, there was a busy A-road to the right, cars zipping by, and quiet reeds to the left. Then a fair amount of greenery appeared on both sides, blocking the road from view and giving the feel of a riverside trail. Or a... coast... path.

A fairly extensive pier arrangement appeared to the left. It looked like someone had a couple of garages full of "pier", and just kept attaching bits, giving it the appearance of a set of letters on a scrabble board. Reaching the entrance and seeing the warning signs and razor wire, I quickly determined that it was some sort of military apparatus, namely Zeta Berth jetty, which is used for amphibious vehicle training. And then it was gone, 30 seconds later I was back to straight trail with the same sort of view ahead – river, bank, trees, sky and tarmac.

I was beginning to think that it was time to take off my waterproof shorts and coat. I was moving well, doing a fair amount of running, and starting to get a bit too warm. The rain had stayed away for a while, although the sky didn't look entirely like it had made its mind up to not throw a little more water downwards. Ahead, through some bushes, appeared a station platform – the perfect point to stop and whip off those overclothes.

I can't remember if I caught up with Andy, or Andy caught up with me, but either way I remember having a brief chat with him while I was stripping off my shorts and coat on the platform of Instow station. He wasn't feeling as good as he'd hoped but wasn't really sure why – a recurring theme during this North Coast 110 race. He was behind his planned pace and didn't have the energy to get moving any faster, so had resigned himself to plod along, hoping that he'd feel better at some point and start enjoying himself a bit more. He did laugh at my stopping for a pint, though.

Having taken my waterproofs off, a spattering of water descended down from the heavens. Bloody typical.

Thankfully, it was only a very light shower that stopped quickly, and soon after the sky started to look like it might behave for a while.

As the Tarka Trail (and South West Coast Path) was following the line of the disused railway, there were no sharp corners, so after the platform at Instow the route went straight ahead.

So why the bloody hell I turned left up the road, I have no idea.

Well, maybe that's not quite true. At the end of the platform was Instow signal box, and either side of the road were a couple of level crossing gates, with some tracks still laid in the road. I was doing my usual thing of not paying attention to what was right in front of my eyes and completely missed the pedestrian entrance on the right side back onto the straight trail ahead, instead opting to following the sharp left turn onto the road. Which, it turns out, was the route that was also on my watch.

You see, being clever, I'd taken the official GPX for the North Coast 110, looked at it and thought it wasn't detailed enough. So, I dug out my extensive archive of South West Coast Path GPXs, and fiddled around merging stuff together, telling myself that I *must* double check it all before the race.

Ahem. Yeah. Forgot that bit.

To be honest, looking at the OS Map it seems the coast path gives you the option of either route, so I wasn't off-course as such, I was just choosing the longer and slightly more complex route. But, in my defence, it was the one nearer the coast.

Around Marine Parade, under grey clouds, I passed a closed Ice cream van (don't they just go home?) and the Commodore

Hotel. I'd had a chat with a lady on the South West Coast Path Facebook group before the run who said she had a food van outside this very hotel, and I'd talked about calling by to say hi and grab a coffee. Sadly, given the off-season time of year, she wasn't going to be there at the time I passed, but it gave the Commodore Hotel a bit more context in my journey, giving me something to look at and tick off as I passed by.

To my right was Instow beach, and there seemed to be something drawing Top Gear presenters to this area around the end of the first decade of the 21st century. Coming on for 15 years ago, when he still had a full head of hair, Jeremy Clarkson reviewed the new Fiesta… but in typical Top Gear fashion[10]. It involved a bright green Fiesta Mk7 on an LCVP landing craft, a whole bunch of Marines from the Amphibious Trials and Training establishment (not far to come from Zeta Berth just back up the river), guns, explosions, helicopters and more, all set in the water just beyond where I was as well as on the beach over at Crow Point.

After walking along the pavement next to the low stone wall separating me from the beach, and trying to not step in some very large puddles whilst simultaneously avoiding getting run over by passing cars, I spotted a South West Coast Path marker. I took the turn off the road into what looked like the entrance to a car park, passing the Glorious Oyster café/restaurant that was somewhere half way between a portacabin and a building, but looked quite inviting. I might have called in, had it been open.

---

[10] If you're interested, it's Top Gear Season 12, Episode 6. It also has some bloke called Boris Johnson as the guest.

At the end of the road, it opened out into a car park, so I had been right. And I recognised this as the car park that I'd half bared my arse to the general public a year before, which brought a smile to my face as I passed.

All that reminiscing about changing behind a caravan had me following the coast path signs to the left and up towards the coast. As I passed by a cricket ground and the path beneath me turned from tarmac to sand, I reached a gate and had a sudden thought. Despite my lack of sense of direction, I didn't think I was supposed to be here.

12

Unwanted excitement

Friday, 15:38

This was the point where the Tarka Trail and South West Coast Path diverged for a mile or so. The Tarka Trail continue along the old railway track bed, while the coast path headed towards, er... the coast. The construction of the Tarka Trail had used all the tarmac in Devon, leaving literally none left for the coast path section, so not only was it grassy and sandy, but was also a bit undulating. Not hilly, but generally a bit up-and-downy. In any case, harder work than flat tarmac.

The North Coast 110 almost entirely follows the route of the South West Coast Path except for 3 sections, and this was one of them. I zoomed out on my watch map to check I was where I thought I was, which wasn't where I was supposed to be, and after confirming that I was, indeed, where I thought I was and not where I was supposed to be, I turned around.

It was annoying. I hate going back. But I knew from previous experience that the path forward, while not considerably longer, was far more of a pain in the arse than a tarmac track.

A couple of minutes later, I'd retraced my steps and just before getting back to the Tarka Trail I noticed a couple of odd-looking things over to my right, tubular steel structures bringing to mind Crow Point lighthouse. It turns out that these are Instow Front and Rear Lighthouses. They do like keeping things simple here – why bother with bricks, cement and a proper building when you can just bung a few steel poles in a pile and stick a bright candle on top! These two lights worked in tandem to form a leading line which helped guide ships through the channel of the estuary when the front and rear lights were aligned. And they've been there a while – over 200 years in fact, having first been built in 1820 – so I guess the whole stone-building-thing might be overrated… at least at a nice, sheltered location like Instow. I'm not sure a tubular lighthouse would last more than about 5 minutes at Hartland Point.

Onto what looked like an old level crossing, I found my way back onto the Tarka Trail, the path a narrow grey strip running through the middle of grassy fields, a grey sky above and a hill on the horizon in the far distance. For now, it just stretched on ahead, obvious and easy, so I kept up my running/walking strategy. It was still just about working, although I was starting to feel like I wanted to do a lot more walking than running.

Trees came and went alongside the path, and a couple of electricity pylons appeared in the distance, slowly edging closer as I moved along. A little after the pylons was a perpendicular concrete road with railway tracks still embedded. This was the access road to East Yelland Power Station, as explained by a notice board next to the junction.

The coal-fired power station set on land right by the river was officially opened in 1955 and produced a decent amount of electricity through to the early 1970s. Fuel came from the coal mines of South Wales, transported across the Bristol Channel to a specially constructed jetty on the adjacent river Taw. As the coal mines closed and the price of coal rose, the power station made little sense economically and closed in 1984, having run for the previous few years at a tiny fraction of its potential output. Today, the buildings have all been demolished, but the deep-water jetty, used to get coal to the station, still remains.

The next couple of miles were pretty uneventful, just a gentle plod along the narrow trail, a mix of grassy fields, trees, bushes, and farms passing by.

I passed the RSPB reserve at Isley Marsh, then alongside the mud flats of Home Farm Marsh, previously an intensive dairy farm but now restored to natural wetland with a bit of low intensity farming thrown in for good measure. Occasionally, under the embankment of the trail there were tunnels, the obvious dirt tracks on either side giving their locations away. These are known as "creeps", and they let cattle and wildlife move to the drier land when the tide is high in the salt marshes by the river.

As a little patch of tree cover ended, a concrete footbed laid across an iron bridge was just ahead, with a Millennium Milepost next to it showing 3½ miles since Instow, and only 3 miles to Barnstaple – I was getting close!

The bridge crossed Fremington Pill at the location of what used to be Fremington Quay, which in the mid-19th century was considered the second busiest port in the country. You wouldn't know it now – there were a few boats dotted around on the mud, waiting for some water to bring them back to life, and that was about it. There's no real feeling that this was an incredibly busy port, bustling with activity at all hours.

It makes sense though – Fremington is about as close to Barnstaple that a large ship could relatively easily get without risking becoming stuck in the sand, so the deep-water quay was built in the 1840s. It was mostly used for importing coal and limestone from South Wales and exporting clay, but trade dropped, and with the railway being taken out of service in the 1960s the quay was no longer used after 1969.

Across the water and mud of the Taw, some 3 miles away were a set of turbines, a few gently spinning in the wind. Fullabrook Down wind farm has 22 turbines, each capable of generating 3MW of power with 90m diameter blades. Pause for a moment… those numbers are *huge!* I've never really considered the size of these things as they're always in the distance, but if you walked at a reasonable pace, it would take a whole minute to walk from one side of the blades to the other! And 3MW is a considerable amount of electricity, enough to power a little under 1,500 homes. And there are 22 of them! OK, I accept the standard argument of them only working when it's windy, but it's quite often windy around north Devon, so it seems like a good idea, at least on the surface. Personally, I think they look quite nice too.

Very soon after crossing the old railway bridge, I was at the platform of Fremington Station. I was having a moment of running, and as I ran past, I looked over at the café and smiled at the memory of having arrived here last year, the call of nature having risen to an absolute bellow at this point, and thankfully getting them to open the conveniences for me to… well, you don't need me to explain the details!

I didn't have time to play in the pirate themed play park, which was a little disappointing as 5 minutes on the swings would have been a nice, relaxing break from all this bloody walking and running!

The effect of the beer was still noticeable here even after almost an hour-and-a-half and over 7 miles after nipping to the pub. It was keeping my spirits higher, my energy up and not causing any of the tiredness or gut problems that I had been a bit concerned about.

Or maybe it was because I was just about 3 miles from checkpoint 2, which was indoors and had warm food. That thought certainly lifted my spirit!

The path stayed enclosed for a while, a narrow grey strip with trees and bushes either side, the odd bridge over the track a reminder of its railway heritage, then it opened out on the salt marshes of Penhill. The wide, flat green ground that stretched away on the left towards the estuary has been reclaimed for low-density, environmentally friendly grazing and the creation of new salt marshes.

On I went, catching sight of a figure in the distance. They were quite far away, but the path was as straight as can be so I could see a good 5 minutes ahead. The big bridge over the Taw at Barnstaple was clearly visible too, the checkpoint just at the far side, tantalisingly close.

Momentarily, the path widened and there was a tin structure in the middle, like a particularly crap bus shelter. I'm not quite sure what it was for. I don't think it could have been a station, or even a halt – the widened area was just too small, barely long enough for a single railway carriage. Too short, even, for a passing place, assuming the track in this area was single line.

But things like this catch my eye from afar on a straight path and draw my interest and concentration. I wondered about it, made up stories, came up with reasons for its existence. All the while, importantly, not thinking about running. So, whatever it was originally designed for I have no idea, but today, it was a help in making a few hundred metres of Tarka Trail pass by a little easier.

And then the trees came again, as did a corner, some streetlight columns on the path, blue cycleway signs – civilisation!

I took the sign labelled "Braunton/Ilfracombe alternative route" around a curve in the path and onto the big bridge that carried the A361 over the river Taw.

The big bridge was opened in May 2007, just like the Torridge bridge down towards Bideford. But at a mere 409 metres, only about two-thirds the length of its cousin down the river, it probably wasn't even a contender in the much-coveted 1988 Concrete Design Awards. It's still impressive to look at on approach though, and unlike the downstream bridge, I actually got to go *over* this one on foot.

And that's when I met Bea for the first time. I caught up with her on the curved approach to the bridge and we started chatting a bit, although the noise of the traffic zooming past on the main A361 a few metres to our right was making conversation a little difficult.

On the far side of the road, the lack of detail on this section of the track on my watch caused a slight problem. The map I was looking at on my little wrist-based screen had a 90-degree right turn just as the road hit the far bank of the river. Looking over to the other side of the busy road, I could see no path, no route through, just solid railings with trees and a steep drop beyond. Bea and I contemplated this for a moment, but luckily she was far better at solving navigation problems like this than I was.

We continued on down the road, ignoring the turn on my watch, and as she'd predicted there was a turn to the *left* which led back around to the way we'd come to eventually go under the bridge. It was obvious really!

At the point where the path met a T-junction, two Climb South West crew members in high-viz jackets clapped us down and directed us left for Barnstaple Rugby Football Club. A turn to the left, all the way around the big rugby club building to the far side and we went through the doors into the hall that was Checkpoint 2.

Checkpoint 2 – Barnstaple	
Distance	**40.4 miles**
Elevation	**5,800ft**
Time	**16:55 – 17:18** (target: 17:08, cut-off: 21:00)
Elapsed Time	**8 hours 59 minutes**
Position	**10**[th]
Split Position	**11**[th]
110 Mile Competitors Remaining: **21**	

There were quite a few crew members in the hall, and as had been the case at checkpoint 1, they couldn't do enough to help.

I went over to the chairs at the back of the hall, stripped off my vest and extracted my walking poles from the Pulse belt before taking a seat.

On the somewhat mentally unchallenging approach to Barnstaple along the straight, flat tarmac trail, I'd been planning what to do when I got to the checkpoint to make sure I didn't waste time. But I'd also decided I'd take 20 minutes, have a little rest, and make sure I got everything done without rushing.

I extracted my mostly depleted, floppy soft flasks from the vest and handed them over to be filled up, water in one and squash in the other.

I'd grabbed my drop bag from the nicely organised selection by the entrance – one benefit of only having 20 or so people in the race at this point was that it was easy to spot your bag. Sat on the seat I opened it up and took out the plastic bag at the top, which contained one of my portable batteries and charge cables. I took my watch off and stuck it on charge on the table, 20 minutes would give me a good few hours more life from the watch. I wasn't sure it was needed given the watch had only gone down about 20% so far, but it was also no effort so worth doing for the peace of mind. Besides, I hadn't really been using the mapping much yet, which drains the battery a lot faster, and I'd definitely need that later in the dark.

Next up, take care of bodily business. I headed round to the toilet, stood in front of a urinal and got on with it. At which point, I wish I hadn't.

Pissing blood is always a bit of a concern. And less than 40% into a long race, that was potentially going to last another 24 hours or more, wasn't the best time to be doing it.

I'd been here before, during the Wendover Woods 50 miler. I was just about to start my third lap, 30 miles into the race, when I nipped to the portaloo and came out somewhat paler than when I'd gone in. I phoned my sister – a doctor – and she suggested that I should probably stop, as we didn't know what was causing it.

I've since had 2 cystoscopies, which is not a procedure I'd wish on anyone once, let alone twice (although maybe it's just me being a bit squeamish about having a camera stuck in my downstairs-area?!). The diagnosis on both occasions was "exercise induced haematuria", which basically means peeing blood because of exercise. A chat with the doctor suggested it's most likely just a bit of the bladder rubbing together during long runs, maybe when empty (so a hot day, not drinking enough is a good trigger), and it's not really anything to be concerned about long term.

So, I opted to do the sensible, grown-up thing and… completely ignore it. If I mentioned it to anyone, I'm out the race. And worse still, I might have to have another fucking cystoscopy! I'd had enough prodding, and nothing bad had been revealed, so I decided that I'd carry on and try my best to forget about it. If the cause was just a bit of dehydration, then next time I had the opportunity to check the colour of my pee it should be fine. Plan sorted. Panic over.

I got back to the seat, trying my best to ignore the whole peeing-blood situation, and had a cup of drink. Then another. And topped up again for a third. A guy asked if I wanted anything, so I took the opportunity to get my first coffee of the race.

Anyone who's read any of my other books knows that I don't have caffeine for a couple of weeks before a race, and then start again part way in, usually early evening, to get some decent benefit. So, this was my re-start of caffeine, and as usual, I was hoping it would pack a punch.

Alongside caffeine, I have a couple of other tricks at this point. I took my first swig of coffee with two paracetamol tablets that I'd broken out of the pack from my drop bag. Pain is inevitable during an ultra – 40 miles so far, quite a long way, and while nothing was acutely sore, things ached. Taking the edge off could only help.

And the other trick – music. I got my trusty little red MP3 player with its 85-hour batter life and a couple of thousand songs pre-loaded – everything from old school Madonna, Bonnie Tyler, Kate Bush, Meatloaf and Dire Straits to much more modern and noisier Enter Shikari, Bring Me the Horizon, Royal Blood and Architects. There's even some Rachmaninoff on there if I'm feeling like something particularly mellow (I'm not a massive classical buff, but his piano concerto number 2 in C minor is exquisite).

My planning whilst making my way along the route over the last hour or so had meant I'd gone through the options of clothing changes, scrapping various choices, and settling on one before I even walked through the door of the checkpoint. I swapped my black long sleeved merino top for an identical one from my drybag that I'd been carrying against my back for the last 40 miles, and replaced that one with a slightly thicker thermal top from my drop bag – this was partly in case I needed it, but mostly to make sure I complied with the compulsory kit. Now I had a nice clean top on, and that always felt so nice in a race!

For the last several ultramarathons, I've gone with the double-sock system including one pair of fiddly Injinji toe-socks inside Saucony Peregrine shoes, and I've ended up with my feet in pieces by the end. To be fair, I think that has quite a bit to do with them getting wet for long periods of time, but for this race I'd decided on a more conventional setup which consisted of a pair of hiking socks I'd proven over 200+ miles of walking last year, inside a pair of roomy but not massively cushioned Altra Lone-Peaks.

What this did mean was that it was easy to change socks. So, I did – another first for me in an ultra.

My feet didn't really hurt – at least not in a way that suggested I wouldn't like what I saw if I took my socks. Shoes off, socks off, feet looked fine, no blisters or even particularly red areas. New socks on, shoes on, again, it felt really refreshing and nice. Definitely something I'll aim to do again.

Whilst doing all this faffing, I was sat opposite Bea and we were chatting about various things, including her shoes. She was wearing a brand I'd not heard of before – Topo – and she absolutely loved them. On her recommendation, I've added them to my list of shoes to take a good look at when I buy some next time.

I had another, weaker coffee, squeezed my fresh water bottles back in my pack and downed the third cup of squash that I'd nabbed from the table earlier.

Time passes quickly in aid stations, and it's easy to lose track, especially when your watch is charging on the table instead of on your wrist. A quick check showed I'd already just passed the 20 minutes I'd allowed myself, so it was time to get going.

Watch back on my wrist, battery and cable back in the drop bag, head torch extracted and set up ready to deploy quickly later when needed and Duran Duran's *Rio* ready to go on my MP3 player (which was the last thing that was playing when I finished the Oner back in April, but I quite fancied now too).

As I headed towards the door, I picked up a home-made Cornish Pasty from the tray that I'd been eyeing up earlier. Four or five hundred calories, all nicely packaged for on-the-go munching – perfect. Getting that sort of energy inside me in a decent mix of carbs, fat and protein would be just what I'd need, and I reckoned if I kept the pace down to a fast walk for the next 20 minutes or so, my stomach would be fine.

I took a look at the TV on the wall by the door, showing the OpenTracking website, all our positions highlighted on a map with little markers. I also saw a few things dotted around on tables which reminded me that here, from this checkpoint in Barnstaple, the 110km race would be starting at 8:30pm, just over 3 hours from now.

As I headed out the door, I wondered how long it would be before someone from that race overtook me?

13

Helicopters and Crows

```
Friday, 17:19
```

I headed out the door, and 30 seconds later headed back in through the door I'd just come out of to check directions. Seriously, I'd come in 25 minutes before, and I'd already forgotten how I got here. I'm an absolute disaster when it comes to navigation!

One of the guys by the door offered to show me the way, not an ounce of annoyance on his face, just totally willing to help. It's the "normal" during an ultramarathon, but it shouldn't go unnoticed – helpers, mostly volunteers, at these events are absolute angels.

Round at the path that joined on to the Tarka Trail he pointed me in the right direction and off I went, happy that I had another few miles of generally straight, un-fuck-up-able navigation to go. Even for me.

Positions get all muddled around in aid stations. People moving slower on the trail can be far more efficient in the checkpoint and head out much earlier, ending up a decent chunk ahead, and vice versa. I was back on my own at this point with no-one visible ahead and no-one behind so far.

But I had a pasty that was absolutely delicious, and some caffeine and paracetamol in my system slowly making their way to wherever they needed to go, and Simon Le Bon telling me that he "can find my own way" in my ear. Alright, don't rub it in, Simon.

I was on the final stretch of the "big detour" along the Torridge and Taw rivers. About 3-and-a-half hours ago, I'd headed south from Appledore down to Bideford, then north and east to Barnstaple. I was now on the final stretch west to a point that, at its closest, was just one mere mile from the path I'd been on earlier. That point was just about another hour-and-a-half away.

None of that bothered me though. As I've said before, just because the route isn't the shortest doesn't really mean anything. It's the coast path, heading along the coast, and that's what you do.

So here I was, fast walking along the side of the river Taw, finishing off that delicious Cornish pasty. The caffeine was obviously starting to take effect, as my walking pace was under 14 minutes for each mile, and I didn't feel like it was any particular effort.

It seems I wasn't quite as in the mood for Duran Duran's *Rio* as I had thought back at the checkpoint, so I fiddled in the side pocket of my vest and liberated the plastic food bag that protected my MP3 player from the rain. I was walking along quickly, and didn't want to slow down, so it was a bit of a faff trying to see through the bag and read the scratched screen, clicking buttons to try and switch music. Once I found the list of artists, I was getting a bit nervous about tripping over something as I wasn't really paying attention ahead, so I picked the first thing I saw – Depeche Mode's *The Singles 86-98*, a decent mix of the first half of their long music career. MP3 player back in my vest, I took a moment to enjoy just walking and looking ahead without feeling like I was going to trip over something as *Stripped* built up in my ear.

A glance behind showed someone coming along, a bit of a way behind but obviously going faster than me on average as I could see a long way back, and they hadn't been in view before. I'd been walking enough, it was time to give running a try – not to get away from the person behind, as I figured they'd likely catch up with me anyway as I would still be walking a fair amount – but more to just try and keep my rate of progress up as high as reasonably possible. Especially as it was still flat, tarmac path, and it was still light. I settled on a ½ mile run, then a ½ mile walk.

After crossing a road, I was passing the fence of RMB Chivenor, which doesn't look that big from the outside, but it's home to 1200 personnel from the Navy, Army and RAF. If you've heard of it before, it may be because the Christmas Number One back in 2011 was 'Wherever You Are' by the *Military Wives and Gareth Malone* – the wives were those of the servicemen from this very base, and the song was created using extracts of their correspondence.

The guy behind was catching up during my walk sections, and as I was passing the base there was maybe 50 metres between us, which seemed a bit silly to me. So, I slowed, and let him catch up.

It turned out to be Chris, who I'd run with at various points along earlier sections. As we were both going at the same sort of pace, had a certain camaraderie having met a few times earlier in the race, and with the descent into night coming soon, we stuck together for a while. It meant I could take advantage of his local knowledge and forget about navigation for a bit, which was always nice.

We were now on the opposite side of the river Taw to the previous section from Bideford to Barnstaple, and the path had a similar feel. A tarmac strip, although this time with a low stone wall on the river side along with the usual trees and bushes to the right side.

And then, a roundabout on the outskirts of Braunton. We followed the road around to the left onto a narrow lane which I immediately recognised as the point of another seminal moment in my walk a year before: my first ever solo wild camp.

Things had gone a bit wrong; I'd covered a lot of miles, was absolutely exhausted and overwhelmed by my inability to find somewhere to settle down. Eventually, through a bit of luck and some help from Eva over the phone, I'd found a grassy spot by Velator Quay. Having reached the spot at night down a dark track and been pleased with how discrete it felt, I hadn't realised until today, as I passed by with Chris in daylight, that from another angle it was in absolute plain sight of the road… no wonder I had kept getting lit up with headlights during the night!

On the walk, I'd arrived at this spot by coming along the toll road from Crow Point, but the correct South West Coast Path route took us up a small set of concrete steps next to the river Caen, over the water outlet of a boundary drain, then around a corner onto a grassy path by the river.

A little way along the neat gravel track, we passed the actual quay area of Velator Quay. Opened in 1870, it was the thriving port for Braunton, with large vessels bringing in coal, limestone, salt, bricks, flour and fertiliser. They would return with clay, potatoes, apples and cider. Like the quay over the water at Fremington, it's surprising to think that all that activity happened here. Today, there's a relatively narrow river, a few picnic benches and some small boats moored.

Passing the quay, we walked fast along the path, passing a solitary house on the right-hand side at the point the toll road to Crow Point came alongside the coast path. With the winding River Caen to our left, the toll road and marshes to the right, we carried on along the flat, easy-going path, chatting away about all sorts of things. The only annoying thing was the wind. The route had been pretty well shielded coming along the Taw towards Barnstaple, but now, heading back west, it had picked up. The gusts didn't so much make it hard work to move, but were just really irritating, constantly blowing in our faces. I decided to put my headphone back in and get a bit more Depeche Mode in my left ear, mainly to stop the wind getting in there.

We came to a junction on the path and headed to the right up a small hill onto an embankment that I recognised from last year as one of the spots I'd thought about pitching my tent. Navigation was easy here – Chris had the local knowledge, and even I knew pretty much where I was going, or rather that there weren't any options to turn off the path for a while, so not much to concentrate on.

I have noticed looking at the maps that the South West Coast Path doesn't actually go along the route that we took – along that embankment by the toll road – but instead takes the curve round to the left, heading further south in an excursion along the path of the river Caen. The official GPX for the North Coast 110, however, shows the same route as the one we took by the toll road, but the instructions don't mention any diversion from the coast path here, although I have spent quite some time looking at the path over the years and I've only just noticed this discrepancy– there are a lot of different lines on the OS map around here!

A little way along the neat, grey gravel track on top of the embankment was a stone stile – essentially a thin but fairly sizeable slab of what looked to be slate blocking the path up to about hip height, a small step underneath. Chris was just ahead of me here, so was first to step over the stile, looking quite uncomfortable as he raised his first leg up and over, and then the other. I didn't find it too much trouble, which was positive. I put it down to the stairgate we've had at home since acquiring the new puppy – I usually can't be bothered to open it, so just awkwardly high-step over it, trying not to smash the mirror next to it with my foot, or fall back down the stairs.

The embankment we were on top of is known as The Great Sea Bank (sounds like something from *Flushed Away*, which, if you haven't seen, you really should), and was built between 1811 and 1815 to hold back high tides and flood waters. To the north side (our right) is Braunton Marsh, and to the left an area isolated by the man-made bank called Horsey Island. There are a series of gravity fed drainage channels and sluice gates, including The Great Sluice (definitely from *Flushed Away*) which is the only point of exit for water to flow into the estuary, and which we walked over the top of after a few minutes on the path.

The embankment ran along for a bit over a mile, and right now we were heading more-or-less straight into the gusty wind, which was continuing to be really quite annoying. The weather forecast had been for that short spell of squally showers mid-afternoon, but once they passed things should have been getting calmer and clearer. It didn't feel like it – although it didn't look like there would be any rain, the constant wind was threatening to blow my hat off, and that would have really pissed me off.

Not having to think about the navigation gave us chance to natter, in between wind gusts at least. We had a good chat about families, work and races, making the passage along that slightly elevated, pretty straight, fairly boring ridge pass with ease using a mix of running and walking. Mostly walking, though, if I remember correctly, apart from when we awkwardly high stepped over a few more of those slate stiles.

The Great Sea Bank dropped down to a road that signalled the end of Horsey Island and led past a house by the water on the left-hand side. This was the White House (no, not that one), previously the Ferry House as the slipway to our left was the site of the old ferry to Appledore. In 1942 it was requisitioned by the war department and used for storage of ammunition and land mines, but now it's a private residence. I hope the war department cleared up properly.

We continued along the road to Crow Point car park, passing through we headed along a further stretch of path and scrub to meet a right turn onto the American Road, so named as it was built by American troops during the war to give easy access to the Taw Estuary while training for the Normandy Landings.

That turn was the closest we would get to Crow Point itself, its somewhat unimpressive lighthouse sat on the edge of the estuary a little under half a mile away to the south. And this was also the closest point we'd get to the trail we were running on earlier, with the top of Northam Burrows being just over a mile away, again due south. Taking the straight route would be boring though... well, maybe not that boring, as we would have to have swum, and I'm absolutely crap as swimming. But it definitely would have been shorter. Having said that, the alternative round-the-estuaries coast path route had meant the total distance we'd covered since Northam Burrows was a little over 25 miles, and that's another 25 miles of those 110 ticked off.

The American Road is long, straight, flat and potholed, and I wasn't entirely looking forward to it, although I knew it was along here that day would turn to night which always brings a sense of excitement. The sun had set about 15 minutes before we turned onto the road, but the sky was still light, the open terrain making the most of the gloaming. One of the things I love about long ultramarathons is the night sections – it's so different to "normal" running, and in the race you get the safety of trackers and support crew as well as the potential of some company as well.

While walking along the early stages of the road, Chris was munching a banana, and I got my head torch out of the back of my pack. I make it sound easy, but it was a minute or two of contorting my body, getting tangled with myself, my pack and the cable for the headtorch, all while trying not to trip in a pothole. Victory was mine, however, and I replaced my hat with my unlit headtorch. I was ready for the night.

The headtorch I use is a Black Diamond Icon, which I've talked about in previous books as I've had it a good few years and used it for quite a few runs. The first time I used it – on one attempt at the Arc of Attrition – I thought it was a bit rubbish, but half way through the race I accidentally found the slightly weird touch-button which turned on the main light, and then I thought it was actually pretty decent (read the manual? Of course not!) However, I had found it a bit inadequate for the grassy trails and wide-open spaces of the Oner and was hoping that it would be up to the job of whatever terrain this race would throw at me.

Behind the fencing to the left and running all the way to Saunton about 3 miles north was all two thousand acres of Braunton Burrows, the largest sand dune system in England, and also, since 2002, a UNESCO International Biosphere Reserve. It doubles as an Army Training area too, a superb playground with dunes rising to 100ft high near the sea!

A little way along the road, the hedges to the left rose, and trees appeared in the distance. The light level had dropped significantly now, and just before we reached Sandy Lane car park it was time to switch on the circle of light that would be my friend and guide for the next 11 or 12 hours.

We passed a turn on the left that went into some deep, dark woods, ignored it and continued on the road. Turns out, that was the right route, but we didn't notice, and instead went through the car park that signalled the end of the American Road. We passed a couple of cars with some subdued activity around them – I couldn't work out whether it was participants in the race sorting out kit changes, or people dogging. It's difficult to differentiate these sorts of things in a secluded car park after dark.

Out the gate at the end of the car park, and now back on the South West Coast Path route after our slight detour, which, incidentally, made no difference to the distance or terrain, it was just the other 2 sides of a rectangle. A little further on the path and we took a sharp right turn by a gate and marker post.

We were now in woods, and I was getting used to the new illumination. With the sun well and truly gone, I was now running and walking in the puddle of slightly off-white light. The problem with light coming from very close to your eyes is that the shadows are cast behind the objects as you look at them, so you get a much more limited sense of depth. In other words, it's easy to trip over. And I was trying hard not to trip over the roots and jutting stones on the ground, which meant concentrating and not really taking in the surroundings.

I remember the woods going on for a while, and then we were in some open patches with slightly undulating, grassy areas to the sides of the track we were on, and some sandy areas visible in patches around – kind of like a golf course. Which is what it was, although not at all obvious in the dark.

This open section took much less concentration as there were no tree roots, and Chris and I were chatting again. He mentioned a bit ahead which he'd met last year when he and his wife did the 110km race.

He told the story. There was a gate, with a "Beware of the Bull" sign on. And, sure enough, there was a bull and a field full of cows. Attracted by a couple of runners with head torches, they all decided to come over and say hello, only in a rapid sort of way that suggested they might cause some trouble. Which ended up with Chris and his wife climbing hedges and having to go on a long, made-up route to get around the cows!

There was an alternative route we could have taken – to go along the road to Saunton Sands, which is actually what I'd done last year due to a navigational error. But I wanted to stick to the true coast path route and talked Chris into going the right way, suggesting that there probably wouldn't be cows in the field again, based on absolutely no knowledge whatsoever. As it happens, the South West Coast Path splits into two here again, so either route is technically valid, but the official race GPX has the "bull field" route.

All that chatter had ended up with us coming to a wooden gate onto a narrow lane. We passed some houses on the right, then hit the main road from Braunton to Croyde.

This was Saunton. But we didn't have time to admire the place, as we crossed the main road onto another narrow lane that began to head uphill.

It had been a while since a significant hill. There were some minor lumps around Appledore, but the last decent hills were before Westward Ho!, almost 30 miles ago. Flat is easier, but it can get a bit dull, and after so many miles of working the same muscles over and over, it can be a beautiful relief in some ways to actually climb a hill. It's still harder work, though. There's no getting around gravity.

The track quickly got dark again after the momentary illumination from the streetlights as we crossed the main road. We followed the track uphill for maybe quarter of a mile before coming to a gate.

Attached to the gate was a sign. "Bull in Field" it proclaimed, in black lettering on a yellow background, with a black outline of a cross looking bull to the side.

So, it was still there, then.

14

No bull, but a Bea

Friday, 19:49

Tentatively, we went through the gate. I haven't been chased by cows and a bull before, but knowing we were entering a field where it had happened at the same time last year was enough to fire up the senses and put me on alert. I kept my torch forward and followed Chris as we climbed the track through the field.

In the distance as we came through the gate was a head torch, presumably attached to a head, which in turn would most likely have been attached to a body and some legs. At least I hope they were, otherwise, someone was probably going to have to fill in some paperwork.

Overall, the climb was about 200 feet up, not huge, and quite gradual, going on for about half a mile through the field. During that time, we managed to catch up with the legs, body, head and headtorch, which turned out to be all in one piece, and called Bea.

Night time in an ultra can be quite a sociable time. If you're racing at the sharp end, then you'll probably stick to whatever plan you've got, but if you're mid-pack and meet up with people doing roughly the same speed as you, then it's nicer to match paces and go along together. Not only does it pass the time more quickly, but it's a bit safer and can also stop you slacking if you're tempted to start taking things a bit too easy.

So, that's what we did. Up to the top of the hill, with a discussion between Chris and Bea, who both had some prior knowledge of this area, about a turn coming up. And then a chat about how they thought it should have been around here, and then how it was back there, and we'd missed it.

We backtracked and took the unobvious (in the dark, at least) left turn at a point that felt like it was some random spot in the middle of a field and started the descent. Through a gate, it stopped being a field, instead there were bushes growing either side enclosing the path. The route was obvious now, although the roots and rocks were back, with the occasional set of steps.

Being downhill, we were all running at this point, and I was at the back, my standard position, given a choice – I much prefer to chase than to lead. There was a right turn, a set of steps which the other two handled with a confidence that had me slightly worried about my own performance, but I caught back up on the flat before we turned another corner to find we had to repay all that downhill with a steep ascent. Bea expressed her discontent with some grown-up words, which made me chuckle. She sounded like my kind of person!

That final turn had oriented us in the direction of the coast, and we carried on through some progressively lighter undergrowth to what felt like a heathland path with bushes either side. To the left, a few metres lower than our position, was the same main road that we'd crossed some time earlier at Saunton.

The path carried on above the road for some time, heading west towards the coast. We were now north of Saunton Sands, with Braunton Burrows, that we'd passed alongside earlier on the American Road, further south still. Curving to the right, we met a set of steps that took us down to the road.

If I'd been on my own, I would have been checking my watch at this point. When you hit this road, there's no obvious indication of which direction to go, at least not that I saw in the dark. There's also no pavement and some blind corners, so the less time you spent on this road, the better.

Luckily, though, I wasn't on my own. Chris led the way without a pause, turning left, and we headed up the road a little way in a line of 3. Thirty seconds and thankfully no cars later, we turned right off the road onto the coast path next to Chesil Cliff House.

I remember this big white building as I passed by this place last year, but Chris padded out the story a little more. The bits that he could remember were that someone had spent a huge amount of money on the house, then got divorced and couldn't complete the build, so it was being sold, at which point Harry Styles was brought up as a potential new owner.

Twelve years. That's how long the project had taken, and it had cost music executive Edward Short £7million… and his marriage. Personally, at least from the photos online, I think it looks like a nice gaff, although a bit pretentious and out of place for the North Devon coast. At the time we were running past, it was on the market for a cool £10million, despite not having a kitchen, bathroom, flooring, or lighting fixtures.

As we continue down the steps, we hit a path that finally felt like the more classic *coast* path again, for the first time since about Westward Ho!. As we headed along the sandy path, the sea splashing against the rocks, Chris glanced back and made an observation.

"I reckon Hitler would have been proud of that," going on to explain how he thought the house looked a lot like a German Fortress.

"Not the sort of accolade you want for your home, is it really?" I replied. He was right though, at least in silhouette: an oppressive black lump, made more sinister with the almost full moon shining out from behind.

The path headed inexorably towards Croyde Bay. By day (and maybe by night?), one of the best surfing beaches in the UK, all I knew was that it was the spot where I'd unexpectedly hit sand last year. Enough sand for it to stick in my memory. And I wasn't looking forward to the trudge across the sand, although, thinking back, it wasn't *that* much sand, was it?

Chris had been reaching down and rubbing his foot a few times over the last mile or two, and as he did it again, he looked to be in quite a bit of discomfort. I asked if everything was OK, and he explained that he had a bunion which had come about after he'd clouted his foot a year ago. It sounded like quite a serious injury, but it all mended, just leaving this lump that was usually not a problem, but today, now, after over 50 miles of coast-pathing, was painful. Fairly low-level pain, but growing all the time, and unrelenting. Bea and I suggested that he have some paracetamol, both of us having them in our packs, but he was reluctant to take any pills and said he'd just work through it.

The path lost its flatness and turned to rocks, a short clamber later we were on the golden sands of Croyde beach, Chris leading the way inland despite his painful foot.

On this beach, you can't just walk along the waterline to the other side of the bay. If you did that, you'd meet a stream running down the beach, and if you carried on, you'd get very wet feet. So, you have to head towards the back of the beach where there's a crossing point over the water, but unless you've been here before – and especially in the dark – it's not very obvious.

I stuck with Chris as we trudged our way across the sand, Bea dropping behind a bit. It got me thinking. I knew that it wasn't particularly far across the sand – maybe 5 minutes – but if you didn't know, it could be a worrisome time right now. I thought of Bea, behind, maybe not knowing how far we had to go, my imagination thinking that she was envisaging miles and miles of sand.

In reality, I was just putting my own concerns onto someone else. I've come to the conclusion that one of the things that makes a great ultrarunner is that they don't give a shit about things that concern… I was going to say "normal people", but, really, I mean "me". They don't think of what might happen next, what terrible terrain is coming up, which bit of their body is aching or could ache, which one of a million things might go wrong. They just… well, they just get on with it. They get the job done, and deal with the problems *when* they arise, not waste time worrying about *if* they might arise.

Anyway, what I'm saying is that I was on the sand worrying about what Bea might be thinking, when she was almost certainly just getting on with the job in hand. One foot in front of the other.

We reached the back of the beach, then followed the edge of the hill around, the path getting narrower… and narrower… to the point where I thought we'd end up in the bloody water anyway if it got any thinner. Just as wet feet seemed inevitable, it widened out and we went through some of that odd, spiky, tall grass that only seems to grow on sand, then on to a concrete "lump" over the water. I think it would be giving it a bit too much credit to call it a bridge.

On the other side of the water, we retraced our steps back out to the bay and headed to what, from memory, I was expecting to be a very short stretch of sand, almost no distance to the road.

It wasn't. It was quite some distance, far longer than I'd had in my head. At this point, I was thinking about how having incorrect knowledge of a route can be worse than not having any knowledge at all!

I could see the road ahead, the point where sand met tarmac. And yet it was never seemed to get any nearer, with every step bringing me seemingly no closer to the road. Trudge, trudge, trudge through the soft, energy sapping sand that took considerable effort and produced very little in the way of results.

But eventually, after what felt like half an hour but was probably only 2 minutes, the sand started to rise, the promise of solid ground just ahead. We came level with a short wall on the right side outside the Beach Café, and I noticed something that looked familiar. A *Refill* point!

Refill is an app, or at least that's how I knew it. But more correctly it's an "award winning campaign from City to Sea to help people live with less plastic". A commendable and thoroughly decent goal, and one which not only saves the planet, but benefits walker and runners alike by having places to fill up your water bottles. Download the app – it's free – and it's got a load of places you can fill up. Not just standalone installations like the one we were next to, but cafes and shops that have signed up and are happy to top up water bottles at no cost.

I backtracked to the water station and pressed the button to see if it worked. A stream of water flowed momentarily down and then headed immediately out towards the sea, seemingly defying gravity. It was being sent there by that one guest on our journey who'd massively outstayed their welcome: the bloody wind.

I was excited though: water! Today was a day where I felt like the more I could get, the better.

I yelled to both Chris and Bea that I was going to fill up my bottles and got on with the job. Soft flasks out of my vest, lids off, up close to the spout so there was a small chance of catching some of the water before the wind blasted it all the way to Cornwall, and then I had two full bottles to last me the next 6 miles to Woolacombe. My excitement was obviously contagious, as unlike Matt and Andy earlier, both Chris and Bea took the opportunity to fill up before we left the beach.

I'd been carrying my pole in my hand across the sand. They're really no use on the soft stuff, they just disappear into it, not really offering anything in the way of assistance. What's more, having had a few delicate things broken by sand over the years, I have a bit of a fear of it near mechanical equipment and I didn't want any risk of the poles not unlocking or failing to lock at some point because of sand in the joints.

But now, on the solid ground of the cunningly named Beach Road, we all clacked our way up, chatting away about what was coming. As we walked, I wiggled my feet around a little in my shoes, checking to see if any sand had made its way past the gaiters. Thankfully it hadn't, another testament to those little bits of fabric on top of the shoes doing a bloody marvellous job!

The next point of interest on the North Coast 110 ultramarathon service from Hartland Quay to Minehead was Baggy Point, a little distance ahead. We were on decent ground that allowed us to walk along at a fast pace, Bea commenting that it was lovely to be "marching" along and making good progress. I got the impression that she usually either ran, or walked fairly leisurely as a recovery, and it was new to be powering along, making good progress while still walking rather than running.

We turned to the left heading up Moor Lane which took us past car parks, camp sites, a surf club (one of the many that make Croyde famous), tea rooms, and a café.

The route took a number of slight slips to the left, the road becoming less *roady* and more *pathy* (those are both definitely words) as we went. We were heading out towards the sea on a point of land, the lights of Croyde were behind us now, to the left across the water was the Hartland Peninsula where we'd started some 13 hours before. It was dark ahead, but three head torches made the path very clear.

Mind you, it wasn't a technical path. It was wide, from memory wide enough for a car to drive along, stony but flat. Not annoying like the Hobby Drive, just a pretty pleasant, easy terrain to move along. To the left, down some cliffs that were getting progressively higher, the sea gently washed against the rocks, bringing us that ever-present, soothing white noise.

Had I not done 55 miles, it would have been a pleasant walk along the coast path. But I had, so I was a little uncomfortable, aching and feeling the miles, but still in good spirits and generally enjoying myself.

Chris, however, was really struggling with his injured foot. The pain was constant, and his gait had changed as he tried not to put pressure on the painful area. He was slowing, happy to continue on, but not at the pace that we had been going, while Bea and I had plenty of energy – at least for fast walking.

He knew what was right for him and seemed happy enough and determined – there was no sense that he was going to stop, just that he was in for a good few hours of fairly slow plodding. After some chatting and more suggestion that he have some painkillers, we said goodbye to Chris then headed on into the darkness.

15

Planet Ultra, where everything is totally fucking weird all the time

Friday, 20:59

Bea and I rounded Baggy point, chattering away, with lots of talk about running. She mentioned that a friend had been helping her, someone that had done this race last year. The ultramarathon community is quite tight and relatively active on social media sites, so I asked who, as I thought there was a vague chance that I might know them. It turns out I did – it was Rodrigo Freeman, who I'd phoned to talk about this race a few months before.

Bea and Rodrigo are good friends, and she spoke very highly of him, both as a runner and just a thoroughly decent human being. With quite a number of high-profile races under his belt – including the 153-mile Spartathlon race, the 305-mile Pheidippides Run and a 48-hour race around a 1km loop – you might expect him to be a little big headed, but he's the humblest guy when you chat, always happy to share his experience and help others. Bea and I were getting quite animated running along chatting about Rodrigo!

The lack of hills over the last 30 or so miles was coming to an end, and the terrain was starting to get a moderate lumpiness to it. Nothing too serious, a bit more undulation, a few minutes of uphill, a few minutes of flat, and few minutes of downhill. All quite pleasant really, using those different muscles, and changing effort levels from a static plod to some moments of higher effort, then moments of easy, floaty descents.

I seemed to be moving faster than Bea on the uphill sections, and I began to pull away on the slope away from Baggy Point. I'd made a decision before starting this race that I wanted to do it at my own pace, to slow when it felt necessary, but also to try and push on if I felt good, even if that meant not having company through the night.

Some way up the hill, I was getting a fairly urgent call of nature having been making the most of my freshly refilled flasks, so after going through a small gate, I glanced back and saw I was a fair way ahead of Bea, her headtorch visible some way down the hill. I turned to the right next to a row of bushes, turned my head torch off (I had no interest in seeing whether I was still peeing blood!), and irrigated the vegetation of North Devon.

By the time I'd finished and turned my head torch back on, Bea was just coming through the gate, slightly surprised to find me hanging around the bushes. I explained what I was up to, which on a normal day (or night) might have been a bit weird, but we were all on Planet Ultra, where everything is totally fucking weird all the time.

The ground levelled off, and we both started running. On the flat and gentle downhills, Bea was strong and just kept going – had I been on my own, I likely would have had intermittent walking breaks along here – I'm a lazy bugger at heart – but she kept me running.

It got me thinking... what was I doing going ahead on the hill earlier? It seemed far more sensible to stick together. I'd keep her company; she'd keep me company. We could help each other through any low points, push on the terrain we were comfortable on and help each other move along.

Bear with me while I go off on a tangent, I promise it's at least slightly relevant...

When you write a book and publish it on Amazon, you get an Author Profile page. You can put blurb on there about how amazing you are (I'm not good at self-praise, I just get sarcastic), and stick a photo of yourself for all the world to see. I uploaded my picture as I was publishing my first book, the one about my walk from Minehead to Penzance, so I used a photo I took on that walk. It's of my stupid face, a blue cap on my head and photochromic glasses that have gone dark. Messy stubble, a blue t-shirt, headphone in one ear and GPS attached to my front. And – here's the relevant bit, finally! – it was taken right where I was in the North Coast 110 race, right now, around Baggy Point. In the background of the photo is Woolacombe Beach, where we were heading.

Sorry, that tangent wasn't really worth it, was it?

Onwards, Bea and I continued along paths, grassy hill to the right, banking down to the left and eventually meeting a drop to waterline. And then we were at a gate, turning left onto a road.

In the dark, it's very difficult to know where you are. Not just the location, but the type of place you are in. When the throw of your headtorch light gives you visibility about one building deep in any direction, it's impossible to tell whether you're in a town (albeit one that forgot to turn on streetlights), or a tiny hamlet of a few houses. Everything feels like the latter when there's no lighting: your world is the bright spot in front of you, cast from your headtorch, with the occasional hint of things a few metres away. That's all. Oh, maybe the odd set of animal eyes randomly too, just to freak you out a bit! So, as we passed a few houses and buildings in Putsborough, I had absolutely no recollection of being here before.

The road then headed to the left, but we ignored that and continued straight ahead past a big white sign for Clifton Court, which seemed to be a bunch of holiday cottages. The path turned from road to something a little less kept, and as the bushes on the left grew taller, the sky unexpectedly and very suddenly decided to dump a load of water on us.

I'm not one to react all that quickly to rain on a run, but this had the feeling of a short but sharp shower. And I didn't want to get soaked. I told Bea to continue on while I got my coat on, and that I'd catch her up. To be honest, with the way she was consistently motoring on I wasn't sure I would, but I intended to try.

I stopped, unclipped and dropped off my race vest, extracted and put on my jacket, then stuck the vest back on. It's not a difficult task generally, but it is made more complicated by the headphone in my ear and the head-torch whose battery pack is on the end of a wire inside the vest. It is a disadvantage of that head torch, a "normal" one wouldn't get in the way of taking my vest on and off. I think I may have to consider getting a new one that that takes easily (and cheaply) replaceable batteries.

Jacket on, race vest back on, head torch eventually back on my head, and headphone dangling down – I'd deal with music again in a minute – I got going on the narrowing path that almost felt like a tunnel with the branches closing over the top.

I kept moving, hoping I'd see Bea's headtorch in the distance shortly. The rain kept coming. My coat did its job, protecting my upper body from the rain, but the downpour was surprisingly heavy and persistent, and my shorts were starting to get wet both directly from the rain and from the water pooling off my jacket. So, before I caught up with Bea, I stopped again, faffed with the drybag and got my waterproof shorts on. At least that didn't involve taking my vest and headtorch off again, and somehow, with another 30 miles in my legs, they felt a little more flexible than when I'd done this back near Appledore.

I got going again, and either Bea had slowed down or I'd found a little burst of speed, because I caught up with her fairly soon after, just as the rain eased off.

I was pretty confident the rain would be a short shower, what with the weather predicting good conditions overnight. I know they can get it a bit wrong, but I'd had a good look at the satellite views the day before and it really didn't look like there was much to come our way once that afternoon band had passed by. I could have stopped and taken my coat and shorts off again now, but I didn't for two reasons. First, I'd just caught up with Bea, and I didn't want to have to do it all over again. And secondly, it gets colder at night – a coat and a second pair of shorts would probably be a good idea… I could see how things went and if I got hot, I'd adjust later.

As we went along the winding path, I was chatting with Bea about how I'd made a mistake on my walk and ended up walking up Marine Drive – a road a little over a mile long that doubles as a car park behind Woolacombe Beach. Only after I'd finished the walk had I realised that the actual South West Coast Path route went along the back of the beach, on a grassy, sandy stretch of trail. I wasn't sure how I'd missed the correct route, so we were both keeping our eyes open for any signs.

As the path turned to road, and the white markings of car parking spaces became visible to our left, I realised we were again on Marine Drive. I assumed that the turn was to the left somewhere ahead to get onto the proper coast path, but despite looking out for it, we didn't find it. After some time, we were fairly convinced we'd gone the wrong way. So… go back and go the right way – which was the same distance, just a little to our left – or carry on and take the first left-turn we could find to re-join the coast path?

We chose the latter. And on reviewing the OS Maps, it turns out things get a bit complicated around there, which might explain why we missed the turn. First, the South West Coast Path splits in two, one way going the route we took down Marine Drive, while the other turns to the left onto the beach. And then the coast path diverts off the drive to join up with its twin on the beach, but the Tarka Trail continues down Marine Drive, re-joining with the coast path towards the bottom. So, technically, we walked a stretch of the Tarka Trail, about 20 or 30 metres to the right of the coast path, as that had the more obvious sign posts, or at least they were the ones we saw.

Towards the bottom of Marine Drive, we found a signpost and headed off the tarmac onto a mix of grass and sand, taking the route down a hill towards a gate at the bottom which led onto the pavement of a road into town.

There were no streetlights to start with, but as we continued down the road and passed the Esplanade car park on the left, we hit the bright lights of Woolacombe town. At the same time, my watch beeped and told me we'd reached the end of its knowledge of this section of the route. Which was annoying, as there was no obvious checkpoint anywhere nearby.

We were within sniffing distance of the checkpoint, but with a junction ahead and about 5 possible directions to take, I started to get apprehensive about how much time we could waste now that I had no route on my watch. I started pressing buttons to choose the next track, which I hoped had the route we'd need to take.

However, I'd forgotten that normal people just open their eyes, and Bea pointed out that there were a couple of people at the junction that looked like race crew. We headed towards them, and sure enough, they pointed us up the hill on Beach Road and told us the hall was no more than "200 yards away".

Two hundred yards... my arse! It was all uphill and went on forever and ever and ever, at least 3 miles.

That's what it felt like anyway. It turns out it was 440 yards, and we went up 100ft. Hardly Mount Everest, but I was very, very ready for the checkpoint and it felt hard work getting there!

Part way up the hill, there was a building with a lot of activity going on and we both assumed that this was the checkpoint.

But as we reached it, we found it was the Methodist Church, and there was some event going on with fairly enthusiastic people going in and out and making a decent amount of noise.

Deflated at not having yet reached our destination, we continued up the hill. I used the momentary disappointment to fire me up and switched into another gear, slightly angrily storming on at a ridiculous walking pace. Eventually, a flapping Climb South West flag came into view, and I turned onto the sloped entrance driveway, down a couple of steps and in through the white front door of Woolacombe Village Hall.

Checkpoint 3 – Woolacombe	
Distance	**60.0 miles**
Elevation	**7,581ft**
Time	**22:07 – 22:26** (target: 23:05, cut-off: 02:00)
Elapsed Time	**14 hours 11 minutes**
Position	**9th**
Split Position	**10th**
110 Mile Competitors Remaining: **20**	

Sometimes, it's not what you get, but when you get it that makes things stick in your mind. A Michelin star restaurant serving a nice plateful of grub might make a nice memory, but it wouldn't be a patch on the pasta with sauce covered in cheese that I had at Woolacombe aid station. At 60 miles into the North Coast 110, it felt like the most delicious meal I had ever eaten!

I was sat on a plastic chair at a white table, holding a recycled cardboard meal box, loaded full of the delicious food. I had a coffee on the table and was alternating between a few mouthfuls of food and a sip or two of coffee.

Bea was sat at the table as well, chatting with two brothers that were helping us – James and Sam Kelly. She knew them well, James being one of her son's teachers. Sam, who spent a lot of time training in the mountains in Europe, had just run his first marathon in around 2 hours 30 minutes, a thoroughly decent marathon time by any account! James had also just run a marathon in a "not great" time which he was hesitant to share, seemingly embarrassed, but we pushed and eventually he told us: 2 hours 45 minutes.

"Oh, that's just rubbish!" we both said, very, very sarcastically – I think in most people's book, a time like that would be the stuff of dreams!

As was a continuing theme, the crew were just excellent again. We wanted for nothing, except maybe another pair of legs, which sadly they'd run out of. Food and drink was brought to us, and water bottles filled without us having to lift a finger.

I fished out another couple of paracetamol to take the edge off the general all-over discomfort that comes with an ultra, it having been more than 5 hours since I has the last ones at Barnstaple. As enjoyable as the food was, I'd made the mistake of eating too much at a race back in April which had led to an unpleasant hour afterwards, so I finished what I had and resisted the urge for seconds. I downed the remainder of the coffee, had a couple of cups of squash to make sure I was nicely hydrated, and got my race vest back on.

Ouch. Strangely, my back hurt quite a bit as I pulled the pack on. It wasn't that uncommon to have a bit of a rub at the bottom of my back after a long race, but I didn't normally notice any issue *during* the race. And this felt bigger, spreading from my lower back up towards my shoulders, quite sensitive and raw. Still, in the scheme of things, it didn't hurt *that* much, and there was sod all I could do about it, so I just ignored it and hoped the pain would disappear once I got moving.

Bea wasn't quite ready yet, but I was more than happy to wait. We had been getting on really well, chatting about all sorts of interesting things and helping each other along the route, it just seemed logical to stick together through the night section.

A minute or two later, ready to tackle the lumpier and generally less populated route to Combe Martin, we turned and headed out the door.

16

A Bull and Seven Hills

Friday, 22:26

The air was cold outside the village hall, not too surprising for a seaside town in Devon at half past 10 on an October night.

Neither Bea or I felt much like running, but the start of the route was downhill, and it would go at least some way towards warming us up after the 20 minutes of being sat still in an aid station. As I started the transition from walking, through half-falling, staggering, then to something vaguely approaching a slow jog, I checked my watch and saw we had just over 14½ miles to go to reach Combe Martin and checkpoint 4. Easy!

At the bottom of the hill, my legs and hips were beginning to warm up and start working properly again. We crossed the roundabout and went along the Esplanade, with hotels, shops and houses to the right-hand side. The race instructions here were to ignore any turns for the coast path as a recent re-route took you an oddly inland way, and instead re-join at the turn by a white hotel. The problem is, under orange streetlights, any light-coloured building looks like a white one, and there were a lot of large, light-coloured buildings. It didn't help that the route on my watch didn't seem quite right, making the navigation here a bit more complicated than I'd hoped.

We crossed the road and went on the pathway closer to the coast through a grass area, re-joining the road a little further along, now much narrower and with fewer streetlights. With the lack of public lighting, I noticed just how dim my headtorch was. I wondered if I this was actually the normal amount of light and I just wasn't used to it yet, having only just moved out of the brighter area, but I soon came to the definite conclusion that, no, it was particularly shit right now.

I'd approached this race not wanting to spend any money – partly due to a tighter financial situation, but also partly because I *always* find something to buy, almost always unnecessarily, and it felt like a part of the challenge to do it without spending anything. It also seemed like a more responsible thing to do – after all, I had several duplicates of everything I'd need, from headtorches to shorts to shoes, all with plenty of life left, so there shouldn't really be any need to buy anything new.

One of the things I typically buy (and it's actually a fairly sensible thing) is a bunch of batteries for my headtorch. I opt for Energizer Lithium – they're lightweight, but more importantly they have higher charge capacity than alkaline batteries, and my headtorch lasts forever with them. Well, usually it does.

The problem with those lithium batteries is that they're bloody expensive, so I dug around at home and found a few that I had left over... just not quite enough of them. So, as I was plodding through the outskirts of Woolacombe, my light was running on 2 batteries that were new, and 2 of questionable heritage, and that question had now been answered. I had a brand-new spare set in my pack, but in the warmth of my living room a week earlier, it had seemed like a good idea to use the mix of old and new and just deal with it if there was a problem. Now, dealing with the problem seemed like a massive pain in the arse.

A little further up narrow road, I spotted a flat area just on the steps of the Mortehoe Apartments and said to Bea that I was going to have to change my batteries. I suggested she go on ahead and I'd catch up, but she was happy to wait around.

Headtorch off, race vest on the ground, batteries out, swap them over, check the headtorch works.

Dead.

I pressed the button again. Nothing.

Oh. Shit.

Again, nothing.

Deep breath, calm down. I've got a spare headtorch if I need it, but I'm sure there's an obvious explanation here.

I opened the battery pack again, took the batteries out and checked they were all in the right way round. They were. I reseated them, and carefully put the lid back on again. Clicked the button and…

YES! Light!

I gave the wire a good wiggle, pulled on the pack lid and generally checked that whatever caused the problem really was fixed and the light was all going to be reliable, and it seemed fine. I don't know what had happened, but it was all working ok now. Phew!

Everything put back away and headtorch – nice and bright now – back on my head, we headed on up the road. The change had cost us just over 3 minutes, but it had felt like half an hour and was enough for me to get a bit cold again.

Almost immediately, we reached a turn for the coast path on our left that I recognised. There was no white hotel on the right, just a tall concrete wall at the back of some parking spaces – I've no idea where I had the idea that there should be a white hotel! We crossed the road and started on one of the many paths that ran over an undulating grassy plain heading into the darkness and out to Morte Point.

I can't remember exactly what we were talking about, but conversation was very easy with Bea. We were chattering away all the time, and it makes the world of difference to how things feel. We delved into some really heavy subjects, both of us having pretty balanced views, and even when we disagreed there was no hints of descending into any arguments.

Distance passed quickly, and soon we were on the interesting rocks of Morte Point. The point, literally translating to Death Point due to the treacherousness of the sea here, has rock formations that almost look like rising waves that were instantaneously turned to stone. Spiky rocks rise up from the ground, both inland and out to sea, with a narrow brown dirt path heading between low rocks that look like stacks of slate on their sides, the layering clearly visible. The grand, otherworldly quality of the point was mostly lost though, as it was just around 11pm.

I remember rounding this point in the other direction last year, the sun shining, blue sky above and suddenly being presented with a stunning view of Woolacombe Sands stretching to the south. Right now, however, it was dark. Rounding the corner of the Morte Point itself, I was met with the sight of… blackness. Except, that is, for the periodic flash of Bull Point lighthouse, beaming out into the night.

I didn't immediately notice the lighthouse, as rounding the point requires a little concentration, especially in the dark. The ground turns from short moor-style grass on a mildly undulating approach to solid rocks, then to that fairly unique slate that comes out the ground at an angle. Imagine a bunch of tiles partly buried side-on in the ground, then round the edges from general environmental wear, and that's what you've got. It's not exactly a trip hazard as the juts out the ground are so close together, but it's the sort of ground that requires some concentration to move across without the risk of face-planting.

Add to that the blackness to the seaward size, and the sense of a drop that was high enough that if you fell over, you'd bounce at least a couple of times off some pointy rocks before the bottom, and you have yourself a recipe for needing to pay attention!

I warned Bea that it was a little technical here but that it didn't last long, and soon we were round the corner, in the dark.

And it really was very dark.

If you look at a map of the north coast of Devon zoomed out a fair bit, you'll see a J shaped bay, the bottom of which runs from Hartland Point east across to Northam, then starts heading up across that one-mile water gap to Crow Point that took 25 miles of walking to get around earlier. It continues up to Croyde and round the prominence of Baggy point, along Woolacombe beach in Morte Bay to Morte Point. At which point, the coastline reaches the very top of the J, takes a pretty much 90-degree turn to the right and continues on a relatively straight line east all the way to Minehead. As we passed around Morte Point, the hill rising from the main body of the promontory blocked all the lovely lights of the previous towns, so it really was, suddenly, pitch black ahead.

The path along here was your classic coast path, the sort of path you imagine when you imagine a coast path, or at least, the sort of path *I* imagine when I imagine a coast path. Narrow, but not too narrow. A bit rocky, but not too much so. The sounds of the sea nearby, somewhere below. Occasional mud, occasional steps. Vegetation to the sides – heather, gorse, that sort of thing, it's difficult to tell at night. The sort of path you can run along while having a chat.

And, oh boy, were we having a chat. Bea and I had been running together for long enough to finish the general chatter about races, training, and that sort of thing. We got onto subjects like nutrition, veganism and corporate greed. The conversation flowed, the emotions rose but mostly because we were both of the pretty much the same viewpoint and thought people should open their eyes a little. I'm deliberately being a bit careful and vague here, writing about some topics in 2022 is far, far riskier than running blindfolded along a rocky outcrop on a cliff edge!

There was excitement and animation in our discussion, and I was going to say it was a great distraction from running, but as I think back, I don't think that's quite right. It sort-of went along with the running, like it *helped*, rather than distracted, motivated rather than numbed. I remember the ground, I remember the steps and the small hills, I remember us both laughing and getting exasperated at various points, but it all seemed to work together, a symbiotic relationship between physical exercise and enjoyable conversation.

It was a bit of an odd moment for me. I went into this race looking forward to solidarity, the minimal entry numbers meaning I would almost certainly be doing a good percentage of this race on my own. But here I was, having a great time running along with someone else.

We got onto electric cars. While Bea explained what she thought of them, I stayed quiet. Then I mentioned we had 3 as a family (ok, the Twizy is almost a toy, but it's still needs an MOT!) and explained that a lot of media FUD (Fear, Uncertainty and Doubt) is propagated by oil-company funded entities, and she admitted that maybe she should look at the concept again. To be fair, though, they are all ridiculously expensive at the moment, unrealistically so. And with electricity prices having jumped so high recently, the benefit of low running costs has pretty much evaporated too.

Enough pseudo-politics. Back to the race!

We rounded Rockham Bay, passed Rockham Beach and Dunn Sand then the path ran alongside a wall that marked the perimeter of Bull Point Lighthouse.

Our head torch lights picked out an information board about Bull Point, the centre of which proclaimed "You are Here", which, to be honest, we already knew, what with there being a bloody great lighthouse right next to us. The board also told of ship remains visible at low tide on the beach we'd just passed, beautiful rock formations, as well as seals and cormorants. It was all academic though, even if we had known to look out all we would have seen is blackness.

Bull Point lighthouse was originally built in 1879 following more than a dozen wrecks over the previous 20 years. In this area, getting into trouble and sinking generally meant the loss of everyone on board as there was nowhere to escape from the sea. In September 1972, after 93 years in operation, the Principal Keeper reported some worrying ground movement and noticeable cracks opening inside the building, along corridors and in store rooms. Six days later, 15 metres of cliff face crashed into the sea, another great chunk subsiding into the gap causing the partial collapse of the fog signal.

An old light tower was put in place for 2 years to keep the light visible for the safety of passing ships. Work began in 1974 on the replacement building, which was designed and built such that the equipment from the old lighthouse could be reused. The new lighthouse was built further inland, which explains why the tower is situated some distance up the hill and behind the row of keeper cottages that are closer to the cliff edge.

After passing the lighthouse, it was dark again. It's a little difficult to write about the details of these sections of a race. You need points of interest along the way to trigger those memories, and in the dark you're limited to things like steep hills, comical conversation points or sea-sounds that suggest unusually large, precarious drops. I do vaguely remember banging on about there being a valley coming up, judging by the elevation profile on my watch, which I'd become more interested in with nothing else to really look out for.

I kept looking at the lumps and bumps on my watch screen, but it turned out there were quite a few, and every time I thought we'd reached the "big one", another glance at the watch showed it was still to come. When we did eventually reach it, the drop and hill turned out to be not particularly different to any of the others – so much for the data-driven approach to running!

But I knew there was a properly big hill coming – and it really did stand out as a big bugger on my watch if I scrolled a little to the right on the elevation profile. I was trying my best to ignore it though, until we passed through a wooded section, a gravelly track and down a couple of steps onto a narrow road that signalled the approach to Lee Bay. Then I couldn't push that hill off the screen any more.

We continued along the narrow road that felt barely wide enough for a single car. The sound of the sea was getting louder as we dropped and the memories of last year's walk started coming back: a Jaguar driver ignoring local advice and heading up this single-track road, and a stunningly beautiful misty view out to sea. But those were all just memories in my head, because right now, at just about midnight, it was just a road – a pitch black road – through a village – a pitch black village. Where the headtorch beam ended, just beyond the occasional building, there could have been golden palaces, scary monsters, huge mountains or a full 96-piece orchestra. If they were quiet, we'd never have known. It was just a road, there was bugger all else to see.

Seeing isn't everything though, and I could tell we were passing the bay, which marks the end of the locally named Fuchsia Valley. The low wall to the left, and the odd mix of concrete walkways, stones, green algae and seaweed just catching my light when I glanced that way hinted at the expanse of sea just beyond the end of our heavily limited visibility.

Rounding the corner after the bay, we headed a little inland past a massive derelict building. Behind the metal fencing surrounding the front were stone facades with boarded windows on the ground floor and smashed panes on the first. Drainpipes and metal chimneys rose up the sides, part hidden behind young, fast-growing trees that had taken root in the untended soil.

This was the Lee Bay Hotel. It was originally built in the 19th century as a manor house, then ran for many years as a 56-bed hotel but closed its doors in 2009. The building was used for training police dogs for a while but now it's just empty and falling apart.

As we passed, Bea and I were discussing how it looked long abandoned, and it was a shame that buildings like that go to waste when they could be used for housing. Although, to be honest, Lee Bay is a bit in the arse end of nowhere, and if the ex-hotel was full of people, it would probably double the population of the place, much to the annoyance of the permanent residents.

There have been several plans to revitalise the site, but the latest proposed plans by a Cornish developer have met with vehement opposition by the locals, who formed an action group to put forward a more sensitive development. As usual, these sorts of legal disagreements take many, many years to resolve, so I expect it'll stay something of an eyesore on the landscape of Lee Bay for quite some time.

Opposite the hotel was a turn up another road, and this was the route we were to take. We'd climbed up a tiny bit from sea level at the bay so far, now began that big bugger of a hill that my watch had been warning of, the first proper climb for miles up to a little under 600ft.

I know as we climbed this hill there was some separation between myself and Bea, but I can't remember who was in front and who was lagging. I have a feeling that I was motoring up the hill to start with, maybe a little too enthusiastically, because I'm fairly sure that a few minutes into the climb I was struggling, mentally working on each step and leaning heavily onto my poles.

After a little under 15 minutes of climbing, the road turned into a track. A similar time later, much to our relief the ascent started to level off, and we turned from the track onto a path, heading towards the coast. It had taken just under half an hour to cover 1.2 miles from that derelict hotel to the top of the hill overlooking Hazel Bushes Bay, the top of the hill marking the half way point between Lee Bay and the bright lights of Ilfracombe.

The elevation profile on my watch showed a general descent, but I had begun to realise that the tiny line on the tiny screen can't fully represent the details of the terrain. What *looks* like a descent can include a surprising number of uphill sections, and when tired, the speed differential between uphill and downhill can make it feel like you're literally spending half your time climbing.

I was beginning to feel the effects of the race now, a general fatigue, not in any way overwhelming but definitely starting to make its presence known. It's funny, I'd been going for round about 17 hours, and it's now that I decide to say that I'm beginning to "feel it". I'd felt absolutely knackered 15 miles in, was pissing blood at 40 miles, and yet it's only now that I consider myself to start feeling a bit tired.

And it's true. At that 15-mile point, I shouldn't have felt like I did – something was wrong. And it turned out to be a combination of heat and dehydration, at least that's my best guess. Pissing blood… well, as exciting and noteworthy as that is, it's not really an indication of tiredness. So yeah, this was the first point where I felt some semblance of knackeredness beyond what I felt was expected.

It was also 1am, which I reckon had a lot to do with it. I'm not great at night – I like my bed, and I like sleep, and my brain was beginning to get an inkling of the total fuckery I had planned for the next few hours and had decided to try and push a little harder with the suggestion that a cosy bed was a far better idea.

Since turning off the track, the route had started to remind me of some night sections of the Oner route around Abbotsbury from 6 month before – open spaces, grassy fields, firm mud-track descents turning into paths that ran along ridges with gradual drops to both sides. It felt high, I can only assume because there were hints of the sea hitting the land some three or four hundred feet below.

We were in an area called Seven Hills, high up on the outskirts of Ilfracombe. In the distance, there were a couple of head torches. Handy, as we had a beacon to show us which direction to go in, and the path definitely didn't go in a straight line. We seemed to be swerving left and right, generally dropping down, but occasionally climbing grassy tracks over small hills covered in what looked like sheep poo, to then drop down again.

The path started to make its way down the steeper side of the cliff, taking us with it. No more gentle hills on grass, this was a narrow switchback trail of stone and rock, the sound of the ocean beginning to become a dominant feature.

It didn't seem possible that we could keep going down… down… and down some more. But we did. The hill was only a little over 500 feet tall, hardly a mountain, but in the darkness the coast path can work its magic, stretching out ascents and descents to almost impossible degrees.

And then, a little under an hour and just over 2 miles since leaving that derelict hotel in Lee Bay, we turned a sharp corner by a stone wall, and joined a road – the very edge of civilisation… well, Ilfracombe, at least.

What do you do when you've hit the edge of town, the bright lights in the distance drawing you in? Obvious really… you stop, have a brief chat, take up positions on opposite sides of a hedge and have a piss.

17

The Tits

Saturday, 00:58

Last year, I'd had to pay attention in Ilfracombe. The route of the coast path feels like it goes through at least three completely different places. There are hills, woods and grass. There are paths that feel like they're routes through a park, then they seem to sneak under the town, complete with building works and safety fences. There's a quay, with its fishy smells, narrow roads and pasty shops. And there's a bit that feels like a normal town, with a theatre, car parks and busy roads. At least during the day.

The route is a bit of a maze, and I made a few mistakes. And that was in the daytime, with the sun shining, people around, signs that could be seen and the hills of the general direction I was going were plainly visible in the distance.

So, as we headed down the widening path that then opened out to a road into town, I mentioned to Bea that we should probably keep our eyes out and pay attention to the route round here so as not to waste any time with mistakes. I also felt the need to mention that, in the middle of town, is a theatre that is shaped like two cones, and is apparently locally known as "Madonna's Bra", something I'd learnt while writing my book about the walk the other way.

We continued down Granville Road which the path had turned into, to a curve that took us pretty much 180 degrees round to the right, continuing down the hill into town. At a sharp left turn, we passed a truck of some description, with someone that Bea either recognised or noticed was another runner alongside.

At just gone 1am, other people become a bit of a rarity, and people who are in the same "tribe" as you become instant friends - the nutcase runners who've been up for God-knows how long, or the crew supporting them. So, we stopped to have a chat. At this point, I noticed what I think Bea had seen before me – there was a bloke almost hanging off the back of the van. His name was Dan, and he looked to me like a decent runner, in a lightweight vest, short-shorts and having the physique of someone who knew what they were doing in these kind of events… which raised the question of what the hell he was doing anywhere near me at this point. The fact that he looked like he was having a particularly shit time went some way towards an explanation.

I can't remember if it was a flat-bed van, or some kind of 4x4 with its back down, but whatever the vehicle, it was like a fully stocked aid station! Laid out on the back were boxes of crisps, sweets, tubs of savoury food and drinks of all variety – they were definitely prepared and ready to offer the runner they were supporting whatever was needed.

And, despite us not being anything to do with them, the crew were truly typical of most ultramarathon crew in that they offered us our pick of anything. Whatever we wanted, we could have. The kindness of strangers is a lovely thing.

As it happened, we didn't need anything, so we briefly chatted about Dan and wished him a swift recovery from whatever was troubling him so he could at least get on with the race, and we headed off down the hill.

We took a right. I don't know why, but it certainly wasn't because of the track on my watch. We'd left that behind a while back and I had yet to notice.

You know that thing I said earlier about paying attention in Ilfracombe? Well, I'd meant *in the middle* of Ilfracombe. We'd barely even started into the town and had already well and truly buggered it up!

We carried on a little way down the road, the concerned noises coming out of my mouth as I noticed the lack of any track on the screen causing us both to slow, stop, and then try and figure out how to undo this mess without having to go back the way we'd come… up the hill. It wasn't a particularly big hill – and oh boy, did we have some big hills to come - but that didn't matter. We did *not* want to go back.

The Garmin Fenix 6X Sapphire is a great bit of kit, but it can't do everything. The tiny screen and minimal amount of map shown doesn't really help when the course you're supposed to be on is a good few hundred metres away.

We looked back up the road we were on. In the distance was a red purple glow, lights shining against some building.

"Oh look, there's The Tits," said Bea.

"I think I said Madonna's Bra," I laughed!

She was right, but because I could only see a tiny chunk of map on my watch, I wasn't sure if by heading directly towards the lights we'd actually get there, or instead we'd end up guided around some corner we couldn't yet see, our target disappearing into the distance in a different direction. As annoying as it was, I suggested the safest thing to do was that we track back and re-join the path on my watch, figuring out where the hell we'd gone wrong.

We headed back to the turn, up the road and round the corner past Dan and his crew (who never mentioned that we'd gone in the wrong direction…) and continued up to that 180-degree turn on Granville Road.

Partly from the slow progress of heading uphill, and partly from some deep-lodged 13-month-old memory, I noticed a gate at the end of the stone wall edging the road. It was easy to miss at the best of times, so it was no wonder we'd run straight past it earlier. But it was a joy to find it, a solution to the quandary of our error. We were on the right path again!

Through the gate and down a path, we ran right past the Landmark Theatre – or The Tits, as I shall now forever call them – along a short section of the main road and then took a left across a large circular open space with some sort of decorative stonework on the ground that was lost to us in the dark. To the right was a near vertical rock face rising high into the air, and straight ahead the race route narrowed to a dark path lit with occasional lampposts, the area having the look of an urban park.

Loud voices came at us suddenly, and my first thought was that there was a bunch of drunk kids around, judging by the enthusiasm and slurring of the speech. A look around the big open area didn't show anyone.

"Oh fuck, don't you throw up on my bag!" drifted down from above, and a glance up showed a group of maybe 10 or 15 teenagers on a ledge on the top of the hill. Next came the unmistakable sound of someone emptying their stomach, followed by a lot of general excited shouting and swearing. Oh, the good old days of being a teenager, I remember them… just!

It's always a bit concerning when you hear a bunch of people – whatever age – making a racket at that time of night when you're fairly vulnerable, running or walking past looking a bit conspicuous in your silly running clothes and being generally pretty knackered. I don't think Bea was too impressed with the suddenness of the noise, but we both settled fairly quickly once we figured they were both too far out the way to cause any trouble, and too busy cleaning puke off of their gear thanks to one of their number.

While looking at the details for this book, I've been poking around on OS Maps, my GPS track logs and various sources of satellite maps including Google Maps. I have to mention something I found in this exact area, which does appear to be real, although you can never quite tell with Google Maps. If you go to Ilfracombe, and find the Capstone Hill area, switch to satellite view and zoom in a bit (at least with the maps towards the end of 2022) there's a great big "E II R 2022" scribed on the hill. And I mean big – 10-metre-high letters, 40 metres wide, but evenly spaced and well presented - one of many tributes to Her Majesty Queen Elizabeth, who died at the age of 96 on 8th September 2022.

Capstone Hill – the hill those kids were on – was, thankfully, above us, and not on our route. As we ran round what is called Capstone Parade, the coast path was being true to its name and we were right on the edge of the sea. But I can't honestly say that I had any sense of being near water. We were on a tarmac path, with darkness to the left and the stone face of a sharply rising hill to the right. Light was mostly from mine and Bea's combined head torches, with some occasional input from the rather dull lamp post lights. I don't remember hearing the sea, I suspect a combination of conversation, concentration and tiredness was to blame for the lack of awareness of our surroundings.

We came off the end of Capstone Parade onto Capstone Road, and here's another one of those times where having some prior knowledge doesn't always help. While I didn't remember this bit specifically, I know around here was a café, a toilet block, a pub, a shop that sold pizza, and a bakery that provided more than adequate steak pasties. However, that's during the daytime. At night, it's just a bunch of buildings all looking similar under the glow of streetlights. Without the people, the hustle and bustle, and the doors and grates all being shut it felt a very different and slightly confusing place.

Rounding the bottom of the harbour, we turned left past the lifeboat station and started heading into a more marine industrial area, toilets and a closed café on the right, and a huge stack of lobster pots to the left side above the water's edge. The whole place smelt strongly of fish.

There were a few dark cars parked on the right side, and Bea headed towards a figure standing by one of them, which turned out to be her husband, Lewi. She picked up a few supplies and some water, and I took advantage of a water top up as well, then we were off again.

It would be remiss of me to not take this opportunity to point out that just across the water from where Bea and I were faffing around with snacks and water, there was the chapel of St Nicholas, perched on top of Lantern Hill. Originally built in the 14th century, being on the water's edge this chapel maintained a guiding beacon for ships – and it's still shining out a light today, said to be the oldest working lighthouse in Britain. The current lantern is a little over 200 years old, and resides in a small white housing on one end of the building. The chapel was in plain view of our location, but it's another one of those things that I just didn't know about at the time, otherwise I would have been looking over at the beacon and it's 600 year history.

As we headed along the road, we were less talkative. In the last few minutes, I'd noticed Bea's speech sounding a little slurred, like she was absolutely knackered. I asked if she was OK, and she replied happy enough. I know these things can wax and wane, but I kept an eye on her to make sure she was moving along steadily and not looking like she was about to keel over.

It wasn't really all that dark, the combination of headtorches and light from the not-to-distant centre of town seeping across to where we were. Soon it was even brighter as we met some metal fencing, some safety lights and a detour to the coast path route.

Now, I hate detours like this. My watch has a nice little line on it telling me where to go, but then someone puts a metal fence up in front of me so I can't go that way. There's always a sign with a big arrow, clearly showing the new direction to go. There might even be a second one, but once you're well and truly diverted off the course you know, the signs stop and you're left with no route, no help and no bloody clue where to go!

We followed a narrow path between two sets of temporary fences through a well-lit area, then were spat out where about 4 or 5 different paths intersected. We took what looked like the right way but ended up by a couple of massive shutter doors underneath a car park. Retracing out steps to the intersection, it was suddenly more confusing as there were at least 2 levels to the paths, with one visible below us in the trees, making the map on my watch a little less useful.

After a bit of faffing about, some swearing from me, and then concluding that the set of steps we could see going upwards were the only real option heading in anything like the right direction, we went that way. They quickly reached a peak, and then started descending. I was a bit apprehensive here – if I'm going the wrong way, I prefer to be going upwards as then I get to go back down later, and I was far from confident that this was the right route. I didn't want to have to climb up all these steps again in a minute!

But the further we went, the more it became clear that this route merged on a curve with the coast path route on my watch, and shortly after that my stress level dropped right back down again as the arrow on the screen showing our actual position settled down on top of the pink line showing the race route.

One thing that struck me was that these works had been a source of confusion when I did the walk over a year before... so they'd been here, in seemingly exactly the same state, for over 13 months! What the bloody hell was going on here?!

After successfully escaping the maze of construction on the edge of town, we passed Ilfracombe Skate Park and headed into some much darker grassy trails around the top of

Rapparee Cove, almost ending up taking the wrong route which would have led down in the cove itself.

Before Ilfracombe, I'd been paying quite close attention to the elevation profile on my watch, ticking off the peaks and valleys and waiting for the big lumps with a little trepidation, but also knowing that they marked off our progress. Through the town, the route was mostly flat, but I knew now we were coming up to another fairly considerable hill, although at a mere 350ft tall, it wasn't as large as the previous one. And because of that, I hadn't really been giving it much thought.

But after we crossed a dark grassy area, picking the correct route at junctions of flattened grass on the ground purely by the line on my watch, we soon joined the narrow trail up to the iron age hill fort at Hillsborough.

It went up. And up. And up.

Three hundred and fifty feet can seem like quite a long way when you're mentally and physically worn out. The path was a bit muddy with some steep, uneven stone steps and bushes either side occasionally snagging clothes. And I'm not sure if I mentioned, but it went up.

I was ahead and building a bit of a gap between myself and Bea, so I took the opportunity to have a little breather while she caught up. A check of my watch showed that, despite it not being a big hill and us having been on the upward path for what felt like quite a while, we weren't even half way. I kept that information to myself.

I moved on, again building up a bit of a gap, then stopping to see if I could see the lights of Ilfracombe from up here, but I don't remember there being anything visible above the bushes.

My wonderfully accurate memory recalled a reasonably steep zig-zag descent on the other side of the hill, but on tarmac, which would be nicer than this muddy, stony path. Tarmac is boring, but it takes out most of the need to check you're not about to trip over something, making it mentally less taxing – something that becomes increasingly appreciated at this time of night and after so many miles.

Eventually, we reached the top. It wasn't a pointy peak like the top of a mountain, and without the spot on my watch elevation profile I probably wouldn't have known we were at the summit. The path looked the same, the bushes turned to trees and after a little way further along, there was a hint of descent.

Pretty soon, it was considerably more than a hint and as we hit the first zig-zag switchback it was clear we were on the steep slope down.

I was a bit confused though. The tarmac I'd been promising Bea hadn't materialised. Presumably it was just a little further down. Yeah, that must be it, it couldn't possibly be my memory at fault.

We were now in a wooded section of the hill, and that brought roots and far more uneven ground to the party. Down we went, switching direction regularly as the path descended, my poles and arms getting a good work out as I slipped and slid on the masses of colourful fallen leaves and almost tripped on several occasions.

In the middle of the night, a bit over 10 miles since the last stop at Woolacombe, all that jiggling around seems to have kicked my bladder into action, and part way down the hill we did the either-side-of-the-hedge pee thing. As usual, I turned my torch off, not wanting to know if I was producing a stream the recommended colour of "light golden straw", or the distinctly unrecommended "black diet coke".

The path continued to zig and indeed zag its way down the hill, the fabled tarmac still not coming into view. Autumn fallen leaves of all shades red, yellow and green covered the ground, making the going slow as it was pretty much impossible to see rocks or roots jutting up from the ground.

There was a flash of light, and it took me a moment to realise it was actually a flash of dark. I had a niggling suspicion that this meant something but being just before 2 o'clock in the morning it took a moment for the thought to slosh its way to front of my brain. Headtorch - flat battery warning! But it couldn't be mine, I'd only just changed the batteries.

"Bea, is your headtorch battery ok?" I asked. "I thought I just saw a flash."

"No, it can't have been mine. I bought this headtorch because it's got a really long battery life, it'll last the whole race."

I wasn't all that convinced. I thought I recognised the headtorch type, and while it has a decent battery life, I didn't think there were any around that could do a full 11- or 12-hour night and then last potentially a few more hours the next evening (despite the cobblers they spout in the marketing material). But there were no more flashes, and both torches stayed on, so within a minute or so I'd forgotten about it.

After several more twists and turns, pretty much at the bottom of the hill, we eventually found the bloody tarmac. So, apologies to Bea, it turns out my brain actually *is* useless at remembering things!

The path made its way around Hele Bay and then onto another one of many Beach Roads in this race, followed by a sharp left after the main car park that took us on to the A399, your classic English coastal A-road of tarmac, pavement and then a little further on, no pavement, just tarmac.

But honestly, I have no memory of this bit from that night. Google Maps shows me what the road looks like (in the day time at least), and the track from my watch shows me that I was there, but I have absolutely no memory of the place.

I do remember that Bea and I were chattering again, and she was sounding far better than earlier. Either that, or I was now in the same state of tiredness and we both sounded normal to each other, like a couple of drunks late into a night out. Maybe it was the conversation that was distracting me from remembering the details; I don't know exactly what we were talking about, but it was easy and fun talking, plenty of sarcasm, swearing and laughs.

And then there was another flash. This one was unmistakable, a bit more urgent, and most definitely from Bea's headtorch.

"I'm pretty sure that's your head torch. I think we should stop in a sec and change your battery." There was some light about from streetlamps by the road, we weren't under any trees and if we could find a spot on the side of the road to stop it would be easy.

"I, um... I don't have a spare with me."

18

The omnipresent A399

```
Saturday, 02:16
```

I'm not an expert in having everything for every eventuality, but one thing I do take with me on overnight ultramarathons (even when not required by the kit list) is a spare head torch with its own set of spare batteries. This is in addition to the spare batteries for my main head torch, which due to my money-saving-endeavours, I was now using.

Without a head torch, Bea was going to be in trouble. In her pack was a power bank she had intended to use for charging the torch, but that would have taken hours, so it was no good for getting the light back on right now.

There was a small parking area on the side of the road next to the Coastguard Cottages which mark the eastern extent of Ilfracombe parish, and at the back of the parking space was a wooden finger post pointing towards the sea which fitted nicely with the route on my watch. We pulled off the road onto the path and stopped for a moment to sort out the situation. I got out my spare head torch from the back of my vest for Bea to use. If I went significantly through into the second night later today (that's an odd phrase to write, but it was well past midnight now) I would likely run out of batteries in my main light, but even if Bea had my headtorch on all night, I'd still have plenty of power left in the spare set of Lithium batteries I had for the second torch.

While we were faffing, a couple of runners came up the road towards us, bobbing headtorches signalling their approach. As far as I can recall, these were the first racers to catch us, obviously part of the 110K race… at least I bloody hoped so, otherwise there were some people who'd really found their second wind. Either that, or we'd slowed down massively, and that didn't feel like the case. As they passed by, the conspicuous dark blue band across their number confirmed which event they were in, our numbers having the red band for the 110-mile race.

With Bea endowed with a shiny new head torch, or at least one that would work for a while, and her other one on charge in her pack, we continued on past the South West Coast Path marker post and started the descent away from the road down towards the coast.

It was back to being a proper coast path, none of this road nonsense. The path was winding and undulating, narrow and near the water, the sea audible most of the time, but not particularly visible in the dark. There were also plenty of trees, their trunks and foliage a constant feature in our headtorch beams.

The route took up residence on the side of a road, which turned out to be the omnipresent A399. The ground was flatter, but not flat, a varying height jumble of stone wall on the right-hand side protecting us from the masses of traffic on the road in the middle of the night. This arrangement went on for a while, until we took a left, crossed over a few unexpected bigger boulders, and ended up on some worryingly wet sand.

I wasn't expecting this. I didn't remember it from previous encounters, and what the hell were we doing on a beach?

Bea didn't seem phased. I think she knew this area, and immediately started heading toward the bright lights at the right side of the beach, which was on the edge of Watermouth harbour.

After a tiny stretch of road up from the beach, we hit a junction with the one-and-only main road in Devon – our old friend the A399 – directly opposite Watermouth Castle. The "castle" is actually a country house built in the mid-19th century, but it was obviously styled on a castle, being a big, grey square building with turrets. Strangely at odds with the formal look of the place, it's actually now a theme park.

The road had no pavement here, but there was a decent verge on the side. Like good citizens, we were on the right-hand side, heading into the oncoming traffic. Of which there was precisely bugger all, as it was 2:45am.

I took advantage of the flat, easy verge to check my timing chart – the target for Combe Martin was 4:19am. Adjusting for our late start, this meant I should aim to *leave* the checkpoint at 4:45am. Allowing half an hour to eat and faff, I should be looking to get there around 4:15am. A few button presses on my watch and I saw we had just under 3 miles to go, and almost an hour and a half to do it in. Loads of time, that shouldn't be a problem at all. In fact, I was boosted a bit by the buffer we'd built up, although just beginning to be slightly wary of a new level of tiredness building up in me.

The road continued upwards, and no sooner had we passed the main entrance to Watermouth Cove Holiday Park than we were met with a coast path marker post taking us back off the road into the darkness. But it was nice darkness, an easy flat path with big grass areas and nothing to trip over.

And tiny little mushrooms.

"Magic mushrooms!" we both yelled out loud at the same time as out headlight torches found the little caps floating above the level of the grass. This led to much excitement and chatter, and the retelling of stories I'm not going to share here.

As it happens, having done a considerable amount more research on psychoactive mushrooms[11], I don't think they were magic mushrooms. But we didn't know that at the time, and moments of excitement perk things up for a while, helping time and distance pass by.

However, even the excitement of some funky fungus couldn't hide the fact that I was beginning to wane. I'd been moving a little slower than I could for most of the time while paired up with Bea, and up until now had felt like I was running below my potential, not really having to push. Don't get me wrong – I wasn't in any way bothered about that, I was happy to be conserving energy, especially at night when the terrain combined with the darkness – which seems to be such a common feature of night-time – would have caused me an injury or a loss of time through mistakes. Slower was better.

Except, now, slower felt like it was beginning to approach my limit, or rather my reserve of energy was depleting, bring my top speed down to pretty much the speed I was going. It

---

[11] Believe it or not, I love macro photography, especially of little mushrooms which are rife in autumn time in my local area. I like to find out what I've taken a photo of, so have a few books and a bit of ever-growing knowledge on funny fungus.

was starting to feel like I was on the verge of having to actually work to keep moving at this pace.

Around the edge of one of the camping fields, we passed the sign for Broadsands Beach, "Voted the Happiest View in the UK." Last time I was here, it was too foggy to see the beach below. I could have done with some of that happiness right now, but sadly the view was just a mass of blackness this time. Maybe one day I'll be able to witness the happiest view in the UK in all its glory.

The path pushed its way out from under the trees and turned into the Old Coast Road. We passed the Sandy Cove Hotel, then back under trees for a short time, before popping out on… you've guessed it… the fucking A399! With my tiredness growing, I was getting a bit grumpier and was beginning to wonder why we hadn't just got a taxi along the bloody road instead of this in-and-out twiddling.

The pavement-less A399 continued downhill, but the coast path took a road on the left, carrying on descending the hill and following it round a bend to the left, at which point my watch directed us through a wooden gate, off the road and onto another trail.

You couldn't get more than a few hundred metres around here without popping out onto a road (usually the A399) or disappearing back onto a path. At least it kept things vaguely interesting, although, to be honest, when it's dark everything starts to look pretty much the same in the circle of off-white light projected from our heads. In the daylight it would have been pretty obvious that we were descending down to the bay of Combe Martin, and that it wasn't too far away, but without the help of the sunlight there was no hints of where we were in the world.

I was getting a bit desperate to get to the checkpoint. I'd gone from feeling a bit tired to absolutely knackered in the space of a mile or so, and I'd resolved to try and have a short sleep when I got to the hall at Combe Martin, which would be the third thing during this race that I've never done in an ultra!

In our tiredness, the conversation between Bea and myself had mostly petered out, and I found myself pulling ahead on the descending route. As there were quite a few twists and turns, I was waiting periodically to make sure I could catch sight of Bea's headtorch behind to check she was on the right route, although in hindsight I think she knew this area and wasn't going to get lost.

Eventually, at the end of what felt like a very long stretch of road with white walls to my right denoting the boundary of some impressive looking three-storey houses, I reached the entrance to the Parade car park, right on the shore.

Yes! Combe Martin! The edge of Exmoor National Park, and the location of the next checkpoint. Well, it was in the village, at least, and villages aren't big, so it couldn't be far.

I was happy now, but in a weary way. Not excited happy, but relieved happy – relieved that I could have a bit of much needed rest. Not too much mind, but I was really hoping a 20-minute nap would reboot me and give me the boost I needed to get on with the remaining 35 or so miles.

I waited on the corner for Bea, and when she caught up, we started headed round past the beach and along the one and only A399 up to the village hall.

Just up to the village hall.

Up the road. Not far.

I ramped up to my speed-walking pace, knowing the checkpoint would come quicker if I went faster.

The problem with Combe Martin – or specifically the Combe Martin checkpoint on the North Coast 110 - is that the village hall is really quite a long way up the road.

For the first Climb South West North Coast event, the 110km in 2019, the checkpoint at Combe Martin was in the Dolphin Inn, right down near the sea front, pretty much the first building you get to as you start up the road. When the 110-mile event was added in 2020, all indoor aid stations were lost because of Covid restrictions, meaning the checkpoint was actually in the car park, and it was a bloody stormy year! All was back on track for the Dolphin in 2021, but at the last minute they cancelled due to Covid related staff shortages. Luckily the Climb South West team sorted the village hall at short notice, and that's stuck as the checkpoint for this year as well.

I knew it was a bit of a way up the road to the hall, but up until this moment – where I was actually just about to start the detour off the coast path to the checkpoint – I'd just assumed that (a) it was only a couple of minutes, and (b) I wouldn't care, as I was almost at the checkpoint and progressing well in the race.

Well, as it happens, I did care. I really, really fucking cared. This was NOT enjoyable. I was NOT having fun.

I was power walking up the road, past pubs, sandwich shops, convenience stores, a car repair garage and quite a lot of houses. I had to swap sides of the road a couple of times as the pavement switched around on the narrow road and, for some inexplicable reason, people were out in their cars in some middle-of-nowhere village at half past 3 in the morning! It didn't occur to me at the time that the cars were almost certainly crew for racers.

I'd made an educated guess that it would be 1 kilometre, or just under 0.7 miles to the village hall from the seafront, based on a vague memory of the map from my what felt now like very inadequate preparation. Every time I looked at my watch – which was far too often – less than 0.1 miles had passed. I was barely over half way, and I felt like I'd been thundering along this bloody, never-ending road for hours.

Still the road went on, past countless more houses, then another shop and post office and a very unique looking pub called the Pack O' Cards. Mostly white but with lots of dark slanted rooves, a plethora of chimneys and plenty of windows and doors, the 17th century inn bore a passing resemblance to a house of cards, and has a history steeped in card-related legends.

On I went, past a car park, a church, a library, and more terraced houses.

And then… finally… 0.83 miles (just over 1.3km) from the coast – and yes, I remembered it from my watch! – there were lights, cars, action! A brown and cream brick building with deep striking red window frames, Combe Martin village hall, in all its glory!

All it meant to me was a place to rest.

Checkpoint 4 – Combe Martin

Distance	**76.0 miles**
Elevation	**11,200ft**
Time	**03:39 – 04:26** (target: 04:45, cut-off: 08:00)
Elapsed Time	**19 hours 44 minutes**
Position	**9th**
Split Position	**11th**

110 Mile Competitors Remaining: 18

I was absolutely, without any tiny shadow of a doubt, completely and utterly knackered. I'd been awake for a little over 24 hours now, covered 76 miles with over 11,000ft of climbing and descent. I'd done this sort of thing before, so I wasn't under any strange illusion that I'd be feeling rosy. But really, I was exhausted.

I couldn't put my finger on why I was quite this tired, mainly because I was having trouble stringing coherent thoughts together. In hindsight, I wonder if the stress and amount of work before the race meant that although I was physically fairly prepared, mentally I was already a bit tired coming into this. For most ultras, I tend to dial back over the week before, start getting in the spirit of the event, planning, panicking, but generally trying to get good sleep and not making the days too stressful. But this time round, it was all-go beforehand. Long days, lots of mentally draining work that leached into the evenings, and not much relaxation at all.

And that was why, after I entered the hall past the very cheerful helper at the door who put a smile on my face (who the hell is that chirpy at 4am?!) and stripped off my race vest, I told the chap that came over to help that I'd like to have a little kip.

I pulled out a chair with the intention of putting my head in my arms on the table to get some shuteye.

"You can go in the room over there if you like," he suggested. "It's dark, which might help."

Good plan. So off I headed, through the big opening (there wasn't a door) into what looked like some kind of function room with a bar at one end. The noise from the main area drifted through, but it was calming – gentle chatter, the odd noise of plates or cutlery on tables, just a light hubbub that would make a nice background soundscape for a nap.

There was nothing in the room. No chairs, benches or tables. But I didn't care – I'd just lay on the floor. I was tired enough; it would be fine. I set a 20-minute timer on my watch – not long, but I figured I'd only need a moment asleep to reset my brain, and if I wasn't asleep within 20 minutes, I wasn't going to happen at all.

I hit the start button on the timer and collapsed fairly ungracefully onto the floor in front of the bar (not the first time that's happened), rolled onto my back and closed my eyes.

My head immediately took on that pleasant, pre-sleep dizziness that you get when you finally lay down and you're exhausted. I was delighted, maybe I was actually going to get some sleep!

I'm not one to fall asleep easily. Little things annoy me – wrinkles in the sheet, the duvet in the wrong place, my pillow a bit twisted, an unusual noise from upstairs, an itch. Almost without fail, my wife falls asleep before I do, which is annoying as she tends to snore, which makes the drift into unconsciousness all the more taxing.

So, although it was annoying, it wasn't altogether surprising when the back of my head against the floor started to annoy me. Then one side of my hip hurt. I rolled onto my side, which made the other side hurt.

I had a brainwave. I got up, almost as inelegantly as when I'd got down, went back out into the main room, and got my pack off the back of the chair I'd hung it over. That would do as an impromptu pillow, and fingers crossed, I'd be able to get that much needed sleep.

Back in the dark room, I was on the floor, pack down on the ground acting as a surprisingly comfortable pillow. All was… well… cold.

I'd been stopped for probably approaching 10 minutes now, and one of things that happens pretty quickly when you've been moving for hours, are tired and it's the middle of the night, is that you get cold. Really cold. Like, shiveringly, teeth-chatteringly, cold.

I tried to ignore it, but it's difficult when your body is involuntarily vibrating on the freezing cold floor.

With 7 of the 20 minutes gone on my timer, I abandoned my plan to sleep, got up and headed back into the main room. I took a seat at an empty table, a bit despondent, resigned to not getting that little snatch of revitalising sleep.

Despite only being in the dark room for a few minutes, the fluorescent lights of the main hall felt surreally bright, the whole hall taking on an other-worldly vibe. I was still shivering sat in the chair, but I was beginning to feel slightly warmer.

The guy who had suggested the dark room and offered to wake me after 20 minutes came back over and we chatted, me explaining that I'd abandoned my sleep idea, it wasn't going to happen. He asked if I wanted anything to eat; there was a kitchen, and he ran through a few food items that I don't remember, until he got to beans on toast.

I don't have beans on toast very often - with my vague attempt at eating a low carbohydrate diet, both of those are a bit above my arbitrary limits. But right now, that sounded *absolutely delicious*. In that moment there was literally no more perfect food I could have imagined.

I wandered over to get a coffee, it seemed like it was probably a good idea. Despite lying on the floor for a bit and sitting in a chair, my walking was pretty decent, almost normal. I've been this far into ultras before, where trying to stand up after stopping has had me looking like some kind of rusty robot, jerking my way slowly across the floor. But this morning, I was walking pretty much normally, or at least that's how it felt. Nothing really hurt. Everything ached, but no muscles or joints were broken. The most annoying thing right then was probably my sore back, unusually rubbed from the race vest.

Back at the table, I cracked out a couple more paracetamol to have with my coffee, and my plate of beans on toast arrived. It was as good as I'd imagined. I hadn't been eating enough, and that was probably a big factor in why I was feeling so tired. This hefty plate of protein and carbs was just what I needed, and I wolfed it down like someone who hadn't eaten for a week.

During the pauses between mouthfuls, I had a look around the hall. Across the table from me was Dan, the guy who was in a bit of a mess back on that road in Ilfracombe. He was talking with his crew about his stomach, saying that it was just hurting so much, and he was going to stop here at Combe Martin. It looked like it was a very tough decision, he didn't strike me as the type of guy who took quitting lightly. He'd been going for a long time in significant discomfort and had reached the end of what he could tolerate.

At the table next to Dan was Bea and her husband, busy organising various bits for the next stage of the race. Bea had a sensitivity to gluten, so had a nutrition strategy that involved staying well clear of it for a month before a race, and then preferring to eat food she'd brought along herself. Lewi, her husband, had parked outside and brought a box with snacks in so she could choose what to eat and pick some bits to take on the next stage through to Lynmouth.

There were Climb South West crew and a few other race participants from both distances (110 mile and 110 kilometre) milling around or seated at tables, somewhere between chirpy and half-dead.

Time, tide, and the North Coast 110 waits for no man, however, and once I'd finished the food, I couldn't spend any more time watching the room, it was time to go.

I got my race vest back on, the now more significant raw patches on my back making it know that they were seriously pissed off with me as the pack slid down over my coat and merino top. I tried my best to ignore it. There was nothing I could do other than get moving, that seemed to make it go away. Sort of, anyway.

I caught Bea's eye as she was prepping to leave, and we exchanged a look that suggested we'd go on out together. She had a new battery for her head torch now, so I headed over to her table to get my spare headtorch back, twisting round and squeezing it into the back of my race vest – there was no way I was taking the vest off and putting it back on again with my back like it was!

Last thing, I went over to the food table and grabbed a packet of crisps, something that has always gone down easily in past ultras, and a banana to stick in my pack, then headed towards the door.

I caught up with Bea, her husband and son and we all headed out into the Devonshire morning.

19

Going down while going up

Saturday, 04:26

At 7:30am, just about 3 hours from the time Bea and I were leaving, 35 runners would set off from Combe Martin village hall on a 55km adventure to Minehead with fresh legs, spirits high, the sun having just risen, bathing the place in beautiful morning light.

At 4:26am, two runners were setting off from Combe Martin village hall on a 55km adventure to Minehead with aching legs, exhausted and sleep deprived, having covered 76 miles over the last 21 hours, and the sun still almost 3 hours away from making an appearance.

I'd already put on my buff and headtorch, and as I was making my way out the door of the village hall, I pulled on my gloves. I was one level above the shivering on the floor earlier, still bloody freezing having been stopped for a while, and although I thought that once I got going, I'd warm up nicely, right now I'd rather have the risk of being too hot than too cold.

Bea and I fell into a rhythm as we made our way down the million-mile (well, 0.83 miles as we now know…) road back to the coast path.

I wasn't particularly happy. I was still tired, and now I didn't have the promise of a snooze in a few miles. Even if there was a stop, I was resigned to the fact that I wouldn't get any sleep. That would have to wait until after I'd finished.

I had 35 miles to go, and 17 hours to do it in. Not a huge challenge on a normal day. On a flat course, I've done that sort of distance in less than 6 hours. But that wasn't when I was hugely tired. And what was coming wasn't flat. Oh no. What was coming next was the tallest hill on the whole of the 630 miles of the South West Coast Path, and that was just the start of the properly lumpy bit. There was round about 7,000ft to clamber over along those next 35 miles.

As the two of us jogged down the road, Bea told me something that to this day I still can't quite believe.

Her husband had just got a parking ticket.

Yes, that's right. I had to double check as well.

A traffic warden had decided to slap a ticket on a car parked on the road outside the village hall. It wasn't a busy road, partly due to it being a sleepy Devon village, but mainly to do with it being FOUR THIRTY IN THE MORNING! Who the hell does that?!

I'm quite a stickler for rules. I get a certain satisfaction when people get a ticket for being a dick – sneakily parking on double yellows or the disabled bay to buy a packet of fags, or getting caught doing 40 on a 30 road past the school.

But when no-one – and I mean *no-one* – is getting hurt, bothered, or even going to notice that a car is parked in possibly a technically incorrect location for no more than 5 minutes at a time where 99% of the population is in bed, I think it's a little bit out of order to be slapping on that ticket. That's just bloody mean[12].

We reached the bottom of the road far quicker than we had got to the top, but there was nothing exciting to look forward to in this direction – certainly no beans on toast. All we met at the bottom was a turn to the right, a little stretch of road, a car park and then onto a road reassuringly called Hangman Path that had a marker for the edge of Exmoor National Park on the verge.

Exmoor, named after the river Exe, the source of which is situated roughly in the middle, is just under 270 square miles of ancient royal hunting forest. A little under a third is in Devon, the remainder in Somerset, and the area is bounded by 34 miles of Bristol Channel coast. The highest point on Exmoor is Dunkery Beacon at 1,703ft, but thankfully it's not near the coast so we wouldn't be going up that high during this race. One other notable thing about Exmoor (at least if you like astrophotography as I do) is that it was designated the first International Dark Sky Reserve in Europe back in 2011.

We'd seen a couple of lights ahead and having now caught up with the owners of them it was nice to meet back up with Andy Mutter. He'd been having some trouble when I'd last seen him and chatted briefly all the way back at Instow, but he seemed to be moving quite well now… unlike me.

As we started up a set of concrete steps, Bea and Andy pushed on ahead up the path. I continued up the steps, the

---

[12] At the time, Bea said that they were going to appeal, but apparently, they didn't take it that far in the end. Bringing it up with Justin from Climb South West got a fairly unsympathetic response – it turns out there was a car park around the back!

path narrowing as bushes and vegetation came in from the sides. I checked the time on my watch – it was 4:38am.

This was it then - the beginning of the climb to the highest point on the South West Coast Path, which also made it the biggest overall climb, bearing in mind we were starting from as near-as-damn sea-level. I continued on with some trepidation.

After being enclosed in greenery for a short while, the path turned to the right and opened out. Bea was ahead, Andy further ahead still – he'd obviously found his legs as he seemed to be storming up the hill.

And it was a proper hill, there was no doubt about that. A hill that went on, and on. And on.

And then on some more.

I was seriously waning. Bea was quite some distance ahead, Andy had disappeared. The path had opened out completely, and it was just a slow slog up a gradual hill on open moorland.

I periodically checked my watch, each time hoping that the little marker on the elevation profile was near the top.

It wasn't.

Somehow, I caught up with Bea. Or, rather, I suspect, she slowed for me to catch up. I told her that there was a cairn at the top, a pretty big pile of stones, to the point where there was no chance of missing the fact that you'd reached the top.

Here, there was no pile of stones, we weren't at the top. So, we had to keep going. Up.

I'm making this sound like a never-ending slog up a mountain, and to be honest, that's what it felt like.

After about a million more years, my head torch light caught a glint of something, and with a few more steps it became more than a glint. Stones. A pile of stones. A fucking great pile of stones! We'd made it!

It had taken just under 50 minutes to walk 2 miles from Combe Martin to the top of Great Hangman. It had felt like 50 hours and 200 miles.

Getting to the top, to the highest point on the whole path, this was cause for a celebration! Or at the very least, a break for 2 minutes.

Bea got her phone out and took a few pics in the dark, including a couple of me posing elegantly by the cairn (yes, I'm being sarcastic). I settled for taking a photo with my mind, the thought of dragging my phone out of the pocket in my race vest and fighting with the touchscreen to try and get the camera to turn on was just too much.

Despite my outwardly happy and delightful demeanour (that one probably doesn't need a sarcasm alert), my mental state was going the opposite way to the terrain. The further up we went, the more down I got emotionally. I had been hoping that once at the top, I'd feel a bit more revitalised, knowing the big hill – the one I'd been dreading – was now out the way. But it didn't seem to work like that. My body was knackered, but not broken, whereas my mind felt like it really, really didn't want any more of this.

A malignant thought had been lingering in my head. It started as a low bubble, not really making itself known, but bringing a certain uncomfortable feeling. And then, as the altitude and tiredness increased, it became clearer and more potent.

At the highest point on the South West Coast Path, the intention clarified, and started to take over my thoughts.

Lynmouth. The next checkpoint. That would do. I'd quit at Lynmouth.

Why?

Oh, that was easy. I did this sort of thing for fun, these long ultramarathons for the enjoyment. Yeah, I loved them! All those miles were brilliant!

Except now.

Right now, it was, frankly, really, really, *really* fucking shit.

I was not only not enjoying it – I was hating it.

It was the almost dawn, I'd been up for some stupid amount of time, and I don't do sleep deprivation. I like my sleep. I want a good 8 hours, maybe 9. Yeah, 9 hours, that sounds good. I hadn't had 9 hours, so this was not good.

What's the point of this shit? It's supposed to be about having fun, not torturing yourself. Why was I doing this? I remembered a conversation with Andy earlier – he wanted to feel better so he could *enjoy* himself. I sure was hell wasn't enjoying myself. I was having a shit time.

There's be no shame in this. I'd done a few decent ultras. I did the Kennet & Avon Canal race a few years before – 145 miles! And this year I'd got the end of the Arc, the Green Man and the Oner, a decent year by any measure. The North Coast 110 was a big ask, and one that was just a bit too much for me.

And ultramarathons that go through the night are a stupid idea, aren't they? I mean, it's difficult enough running a lot of miles, but add in sleep deprivation – which I don't do, did I mention that? – and it's just daft.

No. I'm done with ultras. Last year, I walked a lot of miles on the coast path, and that was far more civilised, far more enjoyable. I could keep the walking up all day, then get some kip at night and start over again. I think, from now on, I'm going to dump the whole through-the-night idea, and go with daytime strolls, taking in the views and enjoying the scenery. This sort of event is a stupid idea.

Bea and I were part running, mostly walking as we descended off Great Hangman and down the 600ft drop to the valley of Sherrycombe. The path was a mix of dirt track and gravelly zigzag as we approached the base of the valley, and then the ascent started on the other side. All the while, the thought of stopping cementing itself in my mind.

As we started to climb up, I opened my mouth.

"I… ", I stuttered. I couldn't quite believe I was going to say it out loud, somehow it felt like it would seal my intention. "I think I'm going to stop at Lynmouth."

20

Beautiful daylight

Saturday, 05:41

We continued on a few steps in silence, the only noise the crunching of the gravel under our feet. I was beginning to wonder if Bea had heard me, or if I'd even said it out loud at all.

"What?! Oh, don't be so *ridiculous!*" came her reply. "I've never heard such nonsense!"

I'm not really sure what I expected. Maybe "aww, poor you, you brave soldier. Well done for giving it a go." That sure as hell wasn't what I got.

"Have your banana," she said, sounding cross.

I felt a bit silly. Like I'd just been told off by my mum. So, without saying anything, I did as I was told. I got the banana out my pack, peeled it and tentatively took a bite, expecting to gag on anything vaguely sweet. The first mouthful went down easily, and the next, and the one after. And soon, I was left wondering what to do with the flaccid banana skin.

The route from Sherrycombe climbed up and over Holdstone Down and then headed on to Trentishoe. My telling off from Bea hadn't turned off my desire to quit, but it had made me start to question it. I think that a lot of the negative thoughts were the result of not having eaten enough, so the banana I'd finished a few minutes before was surely helping with my mental state. And if I really, really used my imagination, I could just about convince myself that there were the very first hints of light in the sky, the beginning of a new dawn.

It was also starting to feel a bit like we were getting somewhere. Soon after leaving Combe Martin, the next place to look forward to – or at least the next place with some relevance that meant I could mentally tick it off – was Trentishoe, a few miles, a few big hills and probably a few hours from the checkpoint. But now, having been over the biggest of all the hills, and now atop the next one, the tracker dot in my mind was slowly but surely making some progress along the route.

What's more, it wouldn't be too long before it was going to get light. Those very first hints of daylight were already visible if you knew how to look for them – mostly out of the corner of your eye, momentarily detecting a faint line at the horizon between land and sky.

Bea and I had started chattering again about various things – the route, the landscape, and the general area. I was coming up to a very significant part of my walk last year, and Bea had run several times around here, so between the two of us (well, mostly Bea if I'm honest), the navigation was in hand without me having to look at my watch. It's a little thing, but it's really nice to just *know* you're on the right route, and not have to keep checking.

We carried on along the path in the growing light, occasionally getting a sense of openness and a drop to the left, but mostly just feeling like we existed within the confines of the twisty stony path that defined our route through Devon.

The path narrowed, the vegetation grew from both sides and became a little harsher, a mixture of gorse and brambles poking from the bushes. Ahead was a small gate, and as we went through, we entered the corner of a fairly sizeable field - one that I immediately recognised, helped by the now significantly increasing pre-dawn light.

The grass of the field rose gently and then dipped away again, a prominent hill in the distance on the far side. In the middle of this field, 13 months before, Chris and I had pitched our tents after the first day of walking from Minehead.

But there was no sleeping here today. Approaching 23 hours after starting the race, there was still a long way to go, no time for a snooze sadly!

We crossed the field, keeping to the coast path route which was alongside the wall on the left side. At various points, you could see clearly over the wall to the nothingness beyond – 200 metres of drop to the sea below, making it pretty clear why the path was *this* side of the wall.

A really, really long race like this one is made easier by being broken down into smaller sections, and it's more about similar time chunks rather than distance. As the distance passes, the tiredness mounts, and the speed buggers off in the other direction, so towards the end, those chunks need to be shorter in distance to take the same sort of time. And that was part of the problem over the past hour or two. We hadn't gone that far, but it had taken a long time, and there was nothing that I could really tick off.

Until now.

This year, or at least this time of year, there was no sign proclaiming "Camping!" as we crossed the stile at the far end of the field, just as my watch told me the sun had risen above the horizon.

There was no blazing ball of fire blinding us though. As we were heading east, the sunrise was very much the wrong side of next valley of Heddon's Mouth... and the rest of Devon and Somerset.

But that didn't stop the morning light being, quite frankly, beautiful. Behind, there were deep blues and indigos, but as you let your gaze drift from west to east across the expanse of the Bristol Channel, the blue lightened and brought in purples, pinks, and hints of orange. The horizon out to sea was peppered with almost black clouds, silhouetted against the light behind. Add to that the contrast against the hills ahead, still dark in the shadow, and we had it was one of those views that makes you thoroughly glad to be out in nature. So much so, that it was *almost* beginning to bring me out of my slump. Almost.

Did I still want to quit? Probably not, not any more. At least not for the same reasons. Given the choice, I'd love to have stopped and put my feet up, as I was, unsurprisingly, absolutely knackered. But I had some semblance of fortitude back, I wasn't going to stop just because I was tired. I had a job to do. It was going to be hard work, but I'd plod on, because... well, that's what you do. I'd paid up, trained hard, and I was going to finish this, no matter what mood my stupid brain decided to get itself into!

Those tick-off points – like the camping field we'd just passed – were coming more frequently now. Heddon's Mouth was just around this next headland, and that had a descent, a bit of a wander along the valley bottom and then an ascent to deal with, then we start getting close to the twin L's of Lynton and Lynmouth, with a few more points to look out for along the way. All made a whole lot easier and more pleasant in the daylight

Now out of the camping field, the path narrowed and got rockier as it went around what I think is the sketchiest point on the whole race route. To the right, the rocks rose almost vertically skywards, great lumps of what looked like granite, and the path was set on a narrow ledge hovering over 650ft above a drop to the sea on the left. To make it a little more fun, there were regular lumps of rock poking onto the path – some the size of house bricks, some significantly bigger. It meant you couldn't just run or even walk along the path, but instead you had to carefully step along to make sure there was no tripping. You really, really wouldn't want to trip here.

I make it sound like we were on the edge of some precarious cliff, but really I think you'd have to make some quite significant mistakes to end up doing yourself an injury. Remember, a lot of people of all abilities walk this path – this section of the path – every day of the year. It still *felt* risky though, carefully threading our way along, wobbling a little from lack of sleep and riding on a pair of legs that didn't inspire confidence.

It didn't last long, and we both survived. In fact, the sense of danger gave rise to a bit of a buzz, a moment of excitement. Rounding the corner, we were faced with Heddon Valley in all its glory, opening up the view to the horizon, bringing much more of that beautiful, multicoloured morning light and a feeling that was actually bordering on joy.

The valley of Heddon's Mouth is part of the West Exmoor Coast and Woods Site of Special Scientific Interest. The scree-clad slopes are home to ancient sessile oak woodland, but lower, where the soil is richer, there is rowan, holly and hazel.

The path ahead was a straight, easy-going path of rough orange stone running between low bracken, ferns, heather and gorse, affording a clear view of the trees covering the river Heddon as it made its way along the valley below.

With my newfound enthusiasm for not quitting just yet, I found the energy to pick up my pace from slow trudging to a decent walking pace. In this state of tiredness, my brain was switching between ecstatic happiness and the depth of despair in minutes, and I was doing my very best to enjoy the current rising mood.

We fell into a sort-of rhythm, me continuously walking at bordering on silly-speed, actually feeling quite good and enjoying myself, while Bea ran on ahead for a bit, then slowed to a far more sensible walking speed where I then caught her again.

The gentle descent of the path soon turned into a steep and twisty, slippery gravel track where we slowed and went down together carefully. I remember at this point chatting about camping adventures. Bea loved the idea of doing that sort of thing one day. Having had one sensible bash at it the previous year, I had some input, and we talked about camping gear, the benefits of various lightweight tents, down and synthetic sleeping bags and all that exciting stuff.

The descent down to the river was quite hard work. The larger gravelly stones slipped around on the dusty surface, especially on the really steep sections, and there were quite a few moments where I thought I was going to be going down part of the hill on my bum. My quads were also seriously disliking the descent, even with the help from my poles, which made my triceps join in the complaining too.

Eventually, the gravel path levelled out as we reached the tree line. The route had been heading away from the coast, down to the river flowing along the valley floor. When we got down alongside, the water was bubbling against rocks and giving the whole place a peaceful, forest glade feel. We followed the marker post pointing us a little further inland to a lovely looking old arched stone bridge.

On the other side of the water, we turned and headed back towards the coast. At a junction with a path rising to the right of the one we were on, there was a marker post which didn't make the correct route immediately obvious. Staying on the path we were on, close to the river would take us to the coast, but the route to the right was such a slight deviation that we couldn't really tell which of the two paths the arrow for Lynton was pointing towards.

If we took the wrong one, we'd add a bit of distance. Not the end of the world normally, but at this point in the race it felt like it could be, so we stopped and debated the merits of each direction.

Down to the coast was most likely wrong, it just felt wrong, but it would be pretty much flat on the return when we found out that it was wrong…

And thinking like that gave us the answer – talking about it out loud, we both decided it was almost certainly the right turn up the hill. We took it, and it quickly turned into a continuous upward climb, less technical than the other side and fairly gentle to the point where I felt like I could maintain the reasonably fast walking pace on the ascent.

"Well, that was surprisingly easy," I said as we rose above the tree line, in front a point where the path disappeared on a sharp turn to the right leaving the beautiful vista out to sea ahead.

"It's not over yet," warned Bea. And as we rounded the corner above Highveer Point, the remainder of the hill came into view. It carried on at a gentle incline along the edge of the cliff for quite some distance, around the rocky outcrop of Great Burland Rocks and into the distance. It wasn't going to be particularly hard; it was just going to be harder than if it was flat!

After the path rounded the Great Burland Rocks, we headed into the combe at Hollow Brook. Looking around on the internet will show you photos of a beautiful waterfall here, and it's quite possible we walked right over the water tumbling down the valley. But I have absolutely no recollection of it at all.

The path curved around the cliffs, climbing a little and then entering an ancient oak woodland with the great name of West Woodybay Wood. The sky had continued to lighten, as it tends to do in the morning, but the sea mist kept the light level subdued, slightly ethereal, and still being early, there were plenty of pink and orange hues. Rounding a corner into the western end of Woody Bay, we caught our first sight of the sun through a break in the trees, an hour since sunrise being long enough for it to have climbed above the headlands in front of us.

And what a view! In fact, Bea said this was one of her favourite views ever, an opinion she'd settled on having been past here a few times before.

The headlands at Crock Point and Duty Point jutted out into the sea, with the stones of Valley of Rocks in the far distance. Still in shadow with the sun behind, the points of land created layers in the mist, beautifully backlit with the morning glow, the layering reminding me of the world-famous Cliffs of Moher in County Clare, Ireland.

Bea took a few pictures with her phone. I was honestly just too tired to be wanting to fight with my sweaty phone to try and make it take a picture, but the view that morning – the colours and the shapes, the sheer beauty of the view and the emotion of the moment – occupies a special place in my brain.

The path continued on through the woods and met the apex of a 180-degree bend on a narrow road, winding its way up from left to right around the corner. The coast path sign sent us down the road, so that's what we did.

After a short time on the road, we took a turn off up a hill back into woods. It was just past 8am now and the sun was well and truly up, but still having a little of the morning orange quality which mixed beautifully with the green trees and multitude of autumn colours across the path.

Off the road, the trail had the feel of the Hobby Drive back near Clovelly – a track that seemed originally meant for horses, slowly curving around into small combes, and then sharply switching back at bridges across flowing water. This place had the intriguing name Hanging Water, but other than hearing the flow of water, I didn't really spot any of it underneath us, let alone any of it hanging.

The similarity to the Hobby Drive had got me thinking back to all those miles and hours... days... months... years... ago. It felt like we'd been going for a lifetime. So many places passed, so many emotions – hot, cold, hungry, thirsty, happy, sad, energetic, tired. And it was far from over yet. We may have covered over 80 miles, but there was still 25 to go – just a marathon or so – but this was not your typical marathon, not one of those where you start fresh and get it done in a few hours.

Soon, we were back out on a very narrow lane called Sir Robert's Path. The lane was barely wide enough for one car, with a small, moss-covered stone wall to the left and a steep drop into the woodland beyond. To the right, moss, fern, and lichen clung to the rocks as they rose steeply upward. Light speckled through the leaves of the trees down on to the ground.

We came to a small junction, and carried on along the now unbelievably narrow road, with just a flimsy looking metal crash-barrier to the left. I really wouldn't want to have been driving down here, and luckily neither, it seems, did anyone else – I'm not sure there would have been anywhere for us to get off the road if we had met a car.

There was a path to the left which very gradually led off the road and down into the trees. It wasn't clear from my watch whether we should continue on the road or take the path, and Bea couldn't remember the exact route. We contemplated for a bit.

If we took the left path, it looked like it had to the potential to head down the steep hill towards the sea. But the road ahead curved around to the right, seemingly the wrong direction. We really wanted to go in the middle of the two, but there were some trees in the way.

It was an event on the coast path, there was a path heading slightly towards the coast, and we were both a bit fed up with the road. So, we took the path.

It sloped gently downwards, nothing too scary. I still couldn't clearly see on the little watch map whether we'd made the right decision, but as the path curved to the left, the descent became steeper and it was now very clear that if we stayed on this route, we'd soon be in the bay below. Which would mean climbing up out the bay a short time later, and I didn't like the idea of that.

"We don't want to be going down," said Bea, echoing my thoughts. Our little foray into the woods had reminded her of the route – or rather reminded her that this was *not* the route we wanted to take. As we'd headed around to the left, it now didn't match up with my watch route either, so we both agreed.

Now we had a choice. Do we backtrack those few hundred metres to the road and then repeat the same few hundred metres back along the road to slightly above our current position. Or do we just turn right and head straight up the hill, through the undergrowth. Well, duh… rules are rules, we sure as hell weren't going back!

It was a steep climb, through brambles and gorse, avoiding trees and occasionally clinging on to branches and anchoring walking poles to make sure we didn't slip back down. But it did only last a short time, and soon we popped out onto the road we'd left less than 5 minutes before.

Did we take the right route by climbing back to the road? Well, yes, but it's one of those South West Coast Path complexities. On some maps, the path appears to only follow the downward route to the bay, along the coast a little and back up – which makes sense, with it being a coast path. But the Ordnance Survey maps show the coast path route splits at that junction of the trail and road that we took earlier, with either route being valid. But, more importantly than all of that, as we continued a little further along the road, it was clear that we were following the route of the official race GPX file on my watch. I'm very glad we took the time to check and end up back on the road – had I been on my own, I could well have ended up over 300 feet below at Crock Point, with a huge, unnecessary climb back up!

21

We found Jesus!

Saturday, 08:25

We were now at the western end of Woody Bay and followed the road around a gradual curve, the view opening up to our left as we descended. The vista took in Lee Bay, with Cuddycleave Wood rising up the hill on the far side, Duty Point tower just poking above the treeline at the summit. In the middle of the picture were grassy fields which ran from where we were all the way along the back of the bay and, edged by a road, ran up past the big white building of Lee Abbey in the distance. Six-acre wood rose on a hill to the right, but we didn't need to worry about that as we'd be taking the road to the Abbey. Even from here, it looked like quite a steep hill.

Chatting away about something I can't remember, we half ran, half walked down the hill adjacent to the shallow valley behind Lee Bay.

I've said this before in previous books, but you'll notice that along the Devon, Cornwall and Dorset coast, there are lots of places with the same name. Back in the olden-days, some chap (almost certainly a chap in the misogynistic olden-days) would have named the bay based on it being windy, pointy, rocky or some other very general feature, unaware that his counterpart 20 miles down the road was doing the same and feeling pretty pleased with himself about his unique choice of name. For instance, we were in Lee Bay, but a few hours before, we were also in Lee Bay back by that derelict hotel on the other side of Ilfracombe.

Lee, as a nautical term, means "sheltered part or side; the side away from the direction from which the wind is blowing." It wasn't particularly windy as we passed by, but I'm not sure that counts as a particularly scientific justification for the name.

The bay is the only easily accessible sandy beach within half an hour's drive of this area, although if you turn up at high tide, you might not spot much sand at all. It's private – part of the Lee Abbey estate – but you can stick the car in a car park, pay a few quid, and enjoy the nice beach, so it's a popular tourist destination.

At the back of the bay, we passed a little coast path marker – as in, it was short, less than a metre tall. It wasn't the first one we'd seen around here either. Maybe the people who put the signs in the ground wanted to save wood? Or there was a rare disease that made all the trees stunted? Or people were particularly short around here? Whatever the case, there was a surplus of diminutive markers in this area.

We were at the bottom of the steep road that cut through the fields in front of us and led to the abbey. Grass either side, edged with wooden posts and wire fencing, the road was narrow – wide enough for one car only, with a few passing places – but well maintained, or maybe just nice and undamaged due to limited traffic. Bea and I made our way upwards, the hill causing a little separation between us as we went at slightly different speeds, me struggling a bit at the back.

I was aware of a noise behind us that had been present for a while, the sound of a revving motorbike or some other small engine. It has been buzzing about in the distance for a while, but the sound was now getting louder, and over the course of a few minutes, my cunningly astute mind starting piecing together the fact that something was coming up the road behind us.

The astuteness was somewhat blunted by coming on for 25 hours of racing and 30 hours of being awake, so the ascending buggy had to decelerate a little as it approached my lumbering form, staggering around in the middle of the road. As I realised, I pulled over to the side and yelled to Bea to keep in, which was wholly unnecessary, as she was a bit more awake than I was and was already tucked in to the side.

The little buggy thing went past, making one hell of a racket. I chuckled as it passed – on the back was a sheep dog. Not sat on a seat or even in some kind of storage area at the back, but just standing on the back, tongue out, ears up, looking like he was loving life.

We continued up to the top of the hill and passed the big stone arched entrance to the Lee Abbey. The buildings on the site have a long history, dating back to around 1200. Originally thought to be a farmhouse built by monks, the Gothic styled buildings seen today were built in the middle of the 19th century. In the early 20th century, the site was extended by two separate companies who both tried to run the place as a hotel, but both went bankrupt. When war broke out, the abbey was used as the location for an evacuated boys' school, and by the time the war had finished the buildings were in a poor state of repair. Over the next 5 years or so, the whole area was repaired by dedicated workers who started the Christian retreat, and some 70 years on, that's what the abbey is known for today.

Last year, when I'd passed in the other direction, I remembered seeing a small wooden post in the middle of the road outside the entrance of the abbey. It was an honesty box for the toll road – very Christian to assume that people would be honest enough to stick a few quid through the box as they drove past.

The honesty box had taken a quantum leap forward in the past year, however. Now, as well as the slot for old-fashioned "cash", there was a contactless card-reader. In 2022, you can be honest using near-field communication, spread-spectrum mobile networks, and quantum tomfoolery on your 21st century mobile device to transfer a couple of quid to the abbey as a token of gratitude for dragging your rubber-wheeled dinosaur burning vehicle over their tarmac.

The buggy that passed us had turned into a field on our right. As the driver pulled up to the gate, the dog jumped off the back, leapt over the fence and ran up to the back end of the field, no hesitation, obviously a well-practiced routine.

Whilst the dog's behaviour was, at least to me, quite amazing – I'd never seen a *real* sheep dog in action, at least not off the TV – there was something else that caught my eye.

I'd found Jesus.

It's pretty common for sheep-farmers (shepherds?) to spray blobs of colour on their stock so they know which of the white fluffy nutcases are theirs. But I'd never seen one with the letters J E S U S sprayed on the side of it. The bona fide Lamb of God!

To be honest, I'm genuinely surprised that the Second Coming was as a sheep. I'm not sure what Jesus Mk 2 is hoping to achieve, as I'm not convinced that all that many people really know of his existence. This time round, I'm don't think there's going to be an Amazon bestseller about how Jesus the Second came back as a sheep and... well, shat all over a field for a while, then ended up as a moderately enjoyable kebab for a few drunken idiots staggering past a local take-away at some time after midnight.

The hill continued up, more gently now, past the entrance to the abbey and the field with Jesus the sheep in, and as we approached the top, the unique and frankly stunning sight of the Valley of Rocks came in to view ahead.

A row of trees ran from left to right a little way ahead of us, but we could see over the top from our higher vantage point. Beyond the trees, taking up most of the view, was the wide-bottomed valley, on the left side a hill, part green with grass, and part grey with granite which dropped away into the sea just beyond. On top were chunks of protruding rock, like miniature tors.

We continued on and reached that line of trees. Passing a stone house on the right, we went through a gate next to a cattle grid which marked the eastern edge of the Lee Abbey estate.

Once past the trees, the view ahead was pretty much entirely the Valley of Rocks. It really is quite unique. If you've never been there, stop reading for a moment and stick "Valley of Rocks Devon" in your Googlapplephonedevice and take a look. Maybe I've had one too many beers as I write this, but

I'm looking at pictures of the area and reminiscing with a sense of wonder at the geological history of this area.

And the goats. This area is famous for goats.

Passing by on my walk in the other direction last year, I saw a sum total of zero goats, but this didn't disappoint me as it wasn't until I was researching for my first book that I found out the area was renowned for the nutty goats.

This year, as Bea and I made our way along the road and hit the big roundabout affair that sits in the middle of the road, marking the point where the foot path heads off the road towards the coast, we saw a *lot* of goats.

And they're aggressive little blighters.

Mostly to each other, mind. They run up and down the hills, and then bash the shit out of each other with their heads. Which, I believe, is what goats are designed to do.

It's slightly disconcerting though, heading through a bunch of animals that you've just watch run in to each other at full force. I was rather hoping not to be knocked off my feet by Billy while I was trying to drag myself along the last quarter of this race.

As I approached, the goats were a bit "Yeah, come on then… you want some?" while simultaneously backing away, the retreat reducing the impact of the threat somewhat.

In any case, by the time I'd processed the fact that charging, headbutting goats might not be something you'd want to get intimately involved with, they were behind us, and we were on a tarmac path on the edge of a pretty sensible (in the sense that it would do you a sensible amount of damage) drop to the left.

Bea was moving well and pulled ahead as I made my way along the path, conscious, and slightly nervous, of the drop to the left. I passed several people, generally opting for the right, land-wards side as I passed, and getting slightly grumpy as a couple walked towards me two astride – or three astride if you count the dog – pushing me towards that edge that I was a little fearful of.

In all honesty, it was another one of those drops where you'd have to turn and run at it with some commitment to fall off, but it *felt* precarious as I wandered along, slightly self-consciously clacking my poles against the tarmac. After all they're supposed to be for tougher, technical terrain, right? I'm not doing Nordic Walking here. Still… they were helping me stay upright, so I was happy to be clacking along.

On the right, Castle Rock passed by, and then Rugged Jack. The path continued round to Ruddy Ball – every placename a joy to the ear… when you research it afterwards. Next time I'm passing, I'll be imparting knowledge of Ruddy Balls and Rugged Jacks to uninterested parties that unwittingly ended up walking alongside someone with just enough knowledge to be dangerous…ly boring.

The path went through some trees then became a narrow road, a parking area to the right making the most of the minimal space by arranging the cars at a sharp angle. There were a bunch of houses on top of a surprisingly tall stone wall to the right, then the wall height dropped, the buildings becoming less precariously balanced on top, and it started to feel like a normal road on the edge of a town. There were still plenty of buildings to the right, but the trees dropped away to the left revealing Lynmouth, Lynmouth Bay and the hills that carried the South West Coast Path east towards Minehead.

The glimpses of the bay were beautiful though. Tall hills to the right, sands fighting with the water where the river met the sea. And down below, Lynmouth. Checkpoint 5. A place to stop and rest a while.

Down. That sounds nice, doesn't it? It's always easy going down…

Bea had gone on ahead at this point, she was moving far better than I was and the checkpoint wasn't far now, so we could meet up again then. The coast path headed off to the left just above the red tile roof of the upper station of the Lynton and Lynmouth Cliff Railway, the world's highest and steepest water-powered railway. Water powered, you (didn't) ask…? Why yes, let me explain.

Build a track up the side of a very steep cliff, slap a cable over a big wheel at the top and dangle two trains off the cables so that one's at the top when the other is at the bottom – this is the principle of a funicular railway. But being first opened in 1890, instead of powering this one with electricity, water from the West Lyn River was piped over a mile to a reservoir at the top of the tracks. Then all you have to do is pop 3 tons of water in the tank under the top train and drop it down the cliff. Simple! OK, there's slightly more to it than that – like brakes. Brakes are quite important. But not much more, it's beautifully simple and having been running for 130 years, it's a great testament to Victorian design and engineering.

The path down is a zigzag, and having walked up it in the other direction, I knew it was quite steep but didn't remember it going on for too long.

I started down. I'd remember correctly - it was quite steep, uncomfortably so. My quads were complaining, and my feet hurt as they bashed into the ground with each step. I still had my poles out, slightly less self-conscious as they were helping absorb some of the impact. At least with it being this steep, it couldn't go on for long.

Ah, padawan. A lot to learn, you have.

I turned the almost 180-degree corner that is the defining feature of zigzag descents to find there was, in fact, plenty of descent to go. And no let-up in the gradient.

As I clattered and banged my way down the slope, I was beginning to become amazed at just how long and how steep a descent this was. I rounded another corner and continued along, passing once more over the tracks of the railway.

Another turn, and at least now I could see the bottom. My feet were beginning to burn from the friction in my shoes, and, despite going down, I was feeling as exhausted as the people had looked finishing the ascent at the top of the path.

It turns out the highest water-powered funicular railway in the world is… well, it's quite high.

As I approached the bottom, I was a little concerned about how much this absolute bitch of a descent was going to smash up my feet. I still needed them for another 20-odd miles of not-insignificantly-hilly terrain, and I could do without them being written off on half a mile of steep tarmac!

Finally, in a state of genuine relief bordering on euphoric, I took the final right turn onto a set of shallow steps that ran down beside the lower railway station, ending on Lymouth Esplanade. On a wall by the steps, a coast-path sign stated that we'd come 1½ miles from the Valley of Rocks, 6½ miles from the Hunter's Inn (a little further inland than we'd ventured into the Heddon Valley), and a surprising 15 miles from Combe Martin.

That got me thinking again... 15 miles. Both a long way, and not far. On a good day, I could run that in significantly under 2 hours, but today, it had taken around 5. And 4 hours ago, I'd been intent on quitting.

That seemed like a distant memory from another time and place, another person even. I certainly wasn't raring to go right now, there wasn't a huge amount of fight left in me, but whilst I may not have wanted to go toe-to-toe with the remainder of the coast path, I was prepared to skirt around behind it, hoping it wouldn't notice as I sneakily made my way to Minehead.

As I turned to the right, I was thinking about how many hours ago, we'd been in the minibus waiting for some guy to try to catch us up in his car, and he'd eventually done so just up the road from here. Andy Quicke's car was in the car park to my left, less than 100 metres away, the memory an odd, ethereal connection to a time both a single day and a thousand years before.

I followed the road adjacent to Lynmouth harbour, passing a metal man constructed of steel rods, a walking pole in one hand, and the other outstretched ready for a handshake with passers-by. 'The Walker' marks the meeting point of the Coleridge Way, the Two Moors Way, the South West Coast Path and the Tarka Trail.

Further along, a fish and chip shop stirred up memories and a huge desire for a plateful of hot food, but sadly it was closed. Just around the corner, whilst still salivating thinking about a nice big piece of cod, I arrived at the Lynmouth Flood Memorial Hall.

Checkpoint 5 – Lynmouth	
Distance	**90.5 miles**
Elevation	**14,500ft**
Time	**09:17 – 09;36** (target: 10:20, cut-off: 13:00)
Elapsed Time	**25 hours 22 minutes**
Position	**10**th
Split Position	**16**th
110 Mile Competitors Remaining: **16**	

The downstairs part of the memorial hall where the checkpoint was located wasn't the height of luxury – just a wooden bench to sit on against the back wall of the single room, a table with a few snacks and nibbles on by the window at the front.

On the back wall were framed information panels detailing the events of 15th August 1952, when a huge storm came in from the Atlantic, dumping an unprecedented amount of rain on Exmoor. The immense downpour led to debris blocking one of the rivers creating a dam which eventually broke cascading water and rocks down into the village. Over 100 buildings were destroyed, most of the bridges washed away from the local rivers and 34 people lost their lives. After the disaster, the river was diverted around the village so hopefully nothing like that will happen again.

I wasn't bothered about the lack of facilities here; I was just happy to stop for a few minutes. And I was hungry. I'd been remembering the last time I was in Lynmouth, eating a hearty portion of fish and chips, then having a rather delicious ice-cream, either or both of which would have gone down an absolute treat right now. Realistically, I knew I wouldn't have time for fish and chips, but I was quietly hoping to grab a pasty from a shop on the way out of town.

For now, though, I was offered a selection of food snacks that at most need a kettle and settled on one of those pasta-mug sachets. A couple of minutes later, I was holding a warm cup filled with a hot, off-white liquid, twirls of pasta visible against the surface as well along with the little bits of unidentifiable stuff that floats around in these things as well.

Bea and her son were sat on the bench to my right, a French guy was to my left, his partner getting him food and drinks.

Bea's husband had gone off to a shop to find some specific food for her as I think some of the supplies were getting a little low, and we both just sat there quietly sipping or eating what we had. I was enjoying the momentary break, but cognisant of the task ahead.

Lynmouth was checkpoint 5 of 6, only Porlock Weir to go before the end. But there was still a little over 20 miles to go, a not insubstantial number of footsteps on aching legs, controlled by an exhausted mind.

But, on the plus side, it wasn't even 9:30am yet, which gave me 12 hours to get to the end. Twelve hours. Whilst that meant I could pretty much crawl to the end and make the cutoff, the thought of taking anything *like* that amount of time filled me with dread. I wanted this over with as soon as it possibly could be.

The chap who'd brought me my cup of pasta came back over and asked if I needed anything else, so I took the opportunity to hand over the standard pair of flaccid soft-flasks for a top up, going with my new "usual" – one with water, one with squash.

I'd finished the pasta and was trying semi-successfully to shove the now full flasks back into my pack as Lewi came back from the shop. There was a bustle of activity to my right, and then I was standing up, wincing again as my pack made its way onto my back. I was starting to get a bit concerned – the distance left equated to quite a few hours, and the pain of my rubbed back wasn't getting any better, in fact it was getting a little worst with every hour that passed. Over the last few miles, it had been moderately painful with each step I took, not just when I put the pack freshly on my back. I wasn't entirely sure how much more I could cope with considering my current, somewhat fragile mental state. But again, what choice did I have? Carry on or quit. And I wasn't quitting, not now.

Pack on, poles in hand, I headed over to the table and grabbed a packet of crisps. I picked up another banana too - it had worked wonders in the night, or at least been partly responsible for getting me out of the almost-quit-pit, and I might need that sort of help again at some point… although I hoped not.

I wasn't exactly feeling ready to tackle the oncoming Devon and Somerset hills, more resigned to it. Bea looked a little more enthusiastic, although Lewi had the look of someone who was concerned about how we were going to handle the next sections. He wished us both good luck in a way that felt really genuine and patted me on the shoulder as we headed out the door. I'd never met this bloke before about 3am that morning, yet it felt like a long-time friend genuinely wishing me the very best.

22

A mismatch of speeds

Saturday, 09:37

My cunning idea of getting a delicious steak pasty was scuppered by the fact that it was October, and I was in Devon. I know coastal towns in this area rely on tourism, but I was surprised at just how closed-up the whole place was, especially considering there were quite a few people around at this early hour on a Saturday morning in October. There would be plenty of shops further into the town, but that was in the wrong direction and I didn't want to detour just to get some food… in hindsight, spending 10 minutes to get some extra nutrition in the form of something I could easily eat, like a couple of pasties, wouldn't have been a poor choice at all.

Out of the memorial hall, we took a right and were soon crossing the bridge over the East Lyn River. Considering there was still about 4,000ft of elevation to cover, the path here was surprisingly flat. Bea and I were wandering along chatting about the course and what was to come. Having previously experienced it in the other direction, where all the ups were downs and downs were ups, I didn't remember any particularly significant climbs or descents between Lynmouth and Minehead. Sure, big parts were up quite high above sea level, but my clever little brain had told me it was just gentle rolling hills, or even that the majority was pretty much flat.

Which was not what Bea was leading me to believe. She told tales of giant, never ending hills – the one we would be climbing soon, and the hill at Bossington being two stand-out brutes.

Oh. My brain couldn't be lying to me, could it?

After the bridge, a nice flat tarmac path took us towards the coast and skirted around *Hole in 1*, the "only 36 hole putting green in the South West". After the golf course, the route headed back inland and then became the type of coast path that we know and love – uneven ground, steps, stones, tree roots… and an inclination to head towards the sky.

The early part of the hill started at a fair gradient, needing a bit of effort, and this highlighted my physical tiredness. Rather than pushing up and feeling the work but being nowhere near my limit like in the early stages of a race, right now it was feeling like a considerable effort just to lift each leg. Had my thinking been less fuddled, I would have recognised that all I really needed was some more food, but neither my stomach nor my brain really gave me any hint that this was the solution to a lot of my problems.

The best I could come up with was to constrain my thoughts just to the top of the hill and remember that every step would get me closer to that point. It was just steps. One after the other. Relentless forwards progress, to nick the phrase coined by Bryon Powell[13].

---

[13] "*Relentless Forward Progress: A Guide to Running Ultramarathons*", by Bryon Powell. I haven't read it, but I probably should.

The path kept climbing up in woods alongside the steep A39 road for a while, then broke out from under the tree cover to a patch of grass. Bea was making great progress as I was waning, and she pulled on ahead up the hill. The distance grew so large that I thought it would be the last time I'd see her in this race.

The path turned to the right, up a couple of stone steps and then onto a single-track path continuing the climb up the side of the hill. People from other races were coming along quite regularly now, and in the open areas this wasn't a problem, but along this narrow path I kept having to step to the side to let people pass. I was going at a snail's pace, so there was no way I wanted to hold people up. Like a good citizen, I was trying to be aware of what was going on behind me but lacking a rear-view mirror I had to keep slowing and glancing behind.

There was a 55k runner a little way behind me, the green band across her number clarifying which race she was doing. Each time I glanced back she seemed to be pretty much the same distance behind, which I thought was a bit odd. She should have been charging past me like the others, but it gave me a little boost to think that even at my glacial pace, I was still moving and making progress, keeping up with (or a staying the same distance) ahead of other competitors.

The single-track path opened back out onto a flatter, grassy area where Bea was waiting for me.

"You shouldn't wait for me," I shouted from a distance back.

"Nonsense, you stuck with me through the night, we'll stick together to the end."

No, that wasn't right. I was going really slowly, and she had a buzzing energy about her. She was smiling, almost skipping along, looking like she was really enjoying herself.

"You can't wait for me; you need to get going. You're doing so well, go on and get this done!"

But she was having none of it and insisted on staying with me. I think she was still a bit worried that I'd quit if left to myself, but that thought had long since gone, or at least bedded down somewhere unnoticeable at the back of my brain. I didn't really *want* to do the rest of the race, I wasn't having much fun, but there was no way I was stopping before the end.

I conceded defeat in the argument for a moment, thinking I'd try again in a minute and wear Bea down eventually, and also trying to find some determination to up my pace a little so as not to hold her back in the meantime.

Contisbury hill is a bit deceptive. The flat area we were on seemed to be almost at the summit. There were higher peaks visible in various directions, but the path appeared to skirt around them and out towards the tip of land that was Foreland Point. But in reality, we were only about half way up the almost 900ft of the hill.

As the climb continued, I started to understand why Bea had spoken of this as one of the big buggers, it really did seem to be unending. Again, I was lagging as she powered on ahead, but she kept stopping to take a photo or just a breather, allowing me to catch up.

Forty minutes after starting the climb, we'd travelled 1.5 miles and *finally* reached the summit of the hill – although it wasn't really much of a summit, just a flat, grassy area where the terrain stopped climbing and mostly levelled off, with hints of a descent ahead.

The path continued around The Foreland and headed over a grassy area, dotted with gorse and heather. Twice more, Bea waited for me as even on the descents I wasn't making very good progress, partly down to my legs but now mostly because of the pain of my vest jiggling against my back. It hadn't been as much of a problem when climbing uphill, but going down caused the pack to bounce, which was getting to be a pretty painful experience with every single footstep.

I caught up with Bea and said again that she should really go on. I could see her beginning to agree, wanting to go ahead, but not wanting to leave me behind. I reckoned she just needed a gently nudge now.

"Come on, you have to go on, I don't want you hanging around." Nicely done, Dick.

"Oh no, that sounded really rude… I mean I don't want you hanging around with me slowing you down!"

She laughed, I think having taken my seemingly blunt statement in the way it was intended, and reluctantly agreed.

"I promise not to quit," I shouted after her as she headed off.

"You'd better not!"

And with that, Bea headed off into the distance.

23

The wrong signs

Saturday, 10:28

Being on my own was actually quite freeing. Don't get me wrong, I'd loved Bea's company and we'd really help each other over the previous 16 hours together, but now I wasn't holding her up anymore which made me feel a little more relaxed. It was just me now, on my own. I could go at my own pace, trudging along, possibly an occasional spurt if I found the energy, and I could just make my way to the end at my own pace.

The path headed downhill – sometimes gently, sometimes less so – through gorse and heather bushes, across grassy areas, the straight line of the horizon as sea met sky a constant presence.

The route was skirting around the land above Foreland Point, the most northerly extent of Exmoor National Park. The path wound gently around on sloping grassland, through patches of heather and gorse. A little further out towards the sea, and about 200ft below my position, was the somewhat precarious looking Lynmouth Foreland Point lighthouse (the Lynmouth being added to differentiate it from another Foreland Point lighthouse in Kent). First lit in 1900, it wasn't a favourite amongst lighthouse keepers as, with its setting on the steep north-facing cliff, you only got to see the sun for 3 months in the summer! As is the way with most of the lighthouses now, it's been automated since 1994, and the cottages are now holiday accommodation.

The coast path had been curving around to the right gently for a while, so it was unusual to hit a sudden sharp left turn onto a set of steps dropping down to a road that was some 600ft below the very top of the hill behind me.

To the left was Coddow Combe, a dry scree and heathland clad valley meeting cliffs at the seaward end. Despite the combe heading directly to the coast, it wasn't the coast path route. Instead, intrepid explorers, we're going to head right. Yes, up the hill.

Onto the road – an odd, lone section of proper tarmac road. After a decent amount of moderately easy descent, I'd recovered some energy, and with good ground under my feet I found a little of my walking speed again. Ahead, towards the top of the hill, there were a couple of racers moving well, presumably part of the shorter races. I had no hope of catching them, my pace may have been a bit quicker than I had been going recently, but it wasn't exactly what you'd call fast.

Coming down the hill towards me were a pair of walkers, I guessed in their late 50s or early 60s. As we met, they asked about the event, having seen the other runners heading past them and obviously singling me out as someone going far slower who'd be happy for chat... which wasn't far wrong.

I stopped, and we spent a couple of minutes talking about how daft 110 miles was (we all agreed on that one, it had just taken 90 miles for me to figure it out), but how maybe the 55km version would be a nice walk, if spread over a day or two. Oh, the idea of a leisurely 55km sounded wonderful...

none of this overwhelming tiredness and unending slog to the end.

Again, I'm making it sound like being 93 miles into the North Coast 110-mile race is literally the worst thing in the world, the sort of thing that you'd be met with in Room 101. And, when you've been awake for 31 hours, it can feel a bit like it. But there's a little part of you inside, the part that tells you to keep going, the bit that got you to enter in the first place, despite having been in this exact mental state many times before, the part of you that loves an *adventure*. That bit… that's the bit that knows you're going to look back at this race, this point now, this lowest of lows, and think it was one of the best times of your life. Brains can be absolutely stupid!

My time on the road soon ended as it turned and carried on in the wrong direction. I headed to the left following a coast path sign back onto the trail, and a little way along, I came to a gate. Next to the gate was a sign:

> If you're walking the coast path,
> you've missed your turn

Clear, simple, obvious – thanks! I assume the sign was there as the owners of Rodney's Farm were fed up with countless navigationally challenged path-walkers wandering across their private land, and it had been helpful in stopping me ending up being another one of them.

I turned around and immediately spotted another racer in the 55k race running towards me, wrongly assuming I knew where the hell I was going.

"Wrong way!" I shouted back, and she silently about turned and started heading back the other way. I was thankful as she was doing the shorter race and was far fresher than I was, so had her eyes open and her brain engaged, at least on the way back from the error she'd just made following me. She spotted a turn off the track onto a path into Gurney's Wood and started off in that direction, which saved me having to engage my brain.

Into the woods, the path wound through another rainforest like area, big ferns, and lots of moss on the lower parts of trees, a wet feel in the air. There were a lot of leaves on the ground, all sorts of autumn colours of yellow, orange, and green, like a rainbow road leading the way into the distance.

My mind was drifting a bit, and I started thinking about all the colours and how they might come about, a nice distraction from thinking about all the parts of me that were hurting. Leaves on the trees are mostly green, but on the ground ahead, the colour seemed to be generally a sort of yellow orange. I figured that leaves fall from the trees when they're getting old, just turning from green to yellow. As they lay on the ground they begin to decay, through yellow to orange to brown, so depending on how freshly fallen they are, the ground will be somewhere between bright greeny-yellow and mulchy, dull brown. As it was early October, things looked quite bright and fresh, a nice light orange.

As pretty as the leaves were, they were also a bit of nuisance on the uneven surface as they hid a multitude of rocks, roots, and holes in the ground, making the going slow and cautious. I really wasn't in the mood to trip over or twist my ankle.

The route ahead was pretty obvious, so poking around on my watch I found the elevation profile to give me some points of reference – the tops and bottoms of hills, that sort of thing.

But as I went along, I realised, again, that the elevation profile on the Garmin watch was just not detailed enough. I'd look at my watch and see the spot in the middle of an ascent – and yet ahead it looked flat, or possibly even downhill. Seemingly 10 minutes later, I'd look again and find I'd hardly moved on the hill. It's not a fault of the watch, more the scale of the event (110 miles) and the speed I was moving (a few miles each hour at most).

What was annoying is that despite realising this shortcoming of the watch, I'd still look forward to the peaks of hills, hoping for a decent bit of descent to come. It's funny, even this late into the race I seemed to think that descending was going to be the easy section, like a nice jog down a gentle hill. In reality, it wouldn't be very nice at all – unsteady legs, nervous brain, tight hips all led to a pretty un-fun experience. In the end, what seemed to happen was that I'd get to the top of the hill, then there'd either be a short, sharp technical downhill that was too steep to go at any sort of pace on, or a little bit of downhill quickly turning into a sharp uphill or a set of uneven steps.

The whole situation was beginning to piss me right off, and I was starting to go down into that pit of despair again. Worryingly, I was starting to talk myself into quitting at Porlock Weir – that felt like a long way away from here, and another 10 miles further after getting there was beginning to feel like too much.

Anyone who's done an ultramarathon knows how ridiculous that would be. Doing over 90% of a 110-mile race, and then quitting because you didn't fancy the last bit. And in the sensible part of my brain, I knew there was absolutely no way in hell the crew at the Porlock Weir checkpoint would let me stop.

The big, oppressive, slightly dark, damp woods carried seemed to go on forever. The first half mile or so was Gurney's Wood, then it became Chubhill Wood, not that I knew or cared what the woods were called or where the arbitrary dividing lines were.

The familiar switchbacks over combes came and went. The ground underfoot continued to be uneven, a little slippery, and with all the trip hazards cunningly hidden under the blanket of colourful leaves.

There are a lot of plant species that are found only on Exmoor, including a couple of whitebeam trees (no I'd never heard of it either), one of which is called Sorbus 'Taxon D', the D standing for Desolate, named after the place that I was currently passing through. There wasn't a lot here other than the trees, so maybe the name fits, but I wouldn't have said it's any more or less desolate than a lot of other sections of the coast path.

Forty minutes after first entering the wooded area, I was heading downhill and deeper inland along Wingate Combe to the point where the path crossed the water. I was just a little above the aptly named Desolation Point, the place name mirroring my current mood.

I needed some cheering up. During the night, I'd got a little fed up with Dave Gahan singing in my ear (unusual, as I normally love Depeche Mode), and as I'd spent most of the night chatting with Bea, I'd discarded the headphone of my MP3 player into a vest pocket. It had crossed my mind a few times over the previous hours to put the music back in my ear, but the effort required to dig out the player and fiddle around on the screen choosing something else just seemed too much.

Right now, though, I was running out of options to cheer myself up, and it seemed like it would be worth a punt – after all, it couldn't make me any *more* pissed off, could it?

The blank screen of my MP3 player confused me initially. Why wasn't it coming when I pressed the buttons? And it dawned on me that maybe, just maybe, the battery was flat. It turns out trying to put music on indeed *could* make me more pissed off!

I've said many times how that little, cheap red MP3 player from Amazon has an amazing 85-hour battery life. Turns out, that's bollocks. It had been playing continuously from when I put it on at Barnstaple the previous evening, but that wasn't even 18 hours ago, let along 85! What a load of old crap, I thought to myself.

In hindsight, it is getting on a bit now at a little under 5 years old, and I've not exactly looked after in terms of charging and storage, just letting it run out after races and charging again months later for the next one. But still, 18 hours is a long, long way from 85 hours.

All the faffing with getting the music player out and putting it away again once I disappointedly realised it was out of power had rubbed the vest around on my back enough to really aggravate it. Every step now led to a sharp pain as the pack bounced just the tiniest bit against the raw patches. I'd been trying not to think about what I'd done to my back, what state it was in, but the pain was beginning to conjure up all sorts of disgusting images in my head that I really didn't want to be thinking about. I tried desperately to change the subject in my mind, to look around and take in the view.

But everything looks pretty much the same in these woods. Ahead, there was a path. Tall trees with dark, damp bark filled the view, their bases covered with mosses. Huge ferns grew periodically from the ground near the trees. The fallen leaves blended together into an autumn orange showing the meandering way ahead. Or behind – if you turned around, the view was pretty much identical.

An hour after entering the woods back near Rodney's Farm, I'd covered 3 miles of wooded path. There were countless ups and downs that didn't seem to appear on my watch elevation profile, but the spot was moving along the screen, making slow but definite progress towards Porlock Weir.

Ahead was a pile of stones that looked vaguely familiar, and as I got closer, I saw the stone cross topping the pile. I had made it to Sister's Fountain.

Having had no idea what this was last year and learning about it when researching the first book, I took the opportunity to have a good look around this time. That's my excuse for why I stopped for a bit, anyway.

If you take a moment to think about the history, places like this are absolutely fascinating. The stones forming the chamber and cross were placed here around 200 years ago. And it's rumoured that Jesus came past here on his way to Glastonbury. Mind you, now we know he's in a field just the other side of Lynton, it's not too much of a stretch to think that one might be true.

Sister's Fountain was one of those spots to tick off on the route to Porlock Weir, so there was a slight uptick in my mood now that I was here. But I'd made something of a mistake in my assumptions of just *where* the fountain was along the route. I'd remembered it being fairly close to Porlock, meaning that I shouldn't have too far to go – maybe a mile or two? Even though a glance at my watch would have set me straight, I somehow stuck with this notion for the next few minutes. Until I passed a sign:

Culbone: 4 miles

Bugger. I knew that the little church at Culbone was this side of Porlock, meaning that I had at least 4 more miles to go. An hour, maybe an hour and a half before I get to the next checkpoint.

A few hundred metres further along the route, I passed another wooden sign:

Culbone: 4½ miles

Oh, for fuck's sake. This is utter bollocks.

To my left was a big, mossy log, and before I had a chance to stop myself, I had sat down, dumped my poles on the floor and put my head in my hands.

24

The more I run, the quicker I'm done

Saturday, 11:46

My head was in turmoil. I knew I couldn't quit, that it would be an unwinnable fight with the checkpoint crew at Porlock Weir, but that didn't stop me wanting to just finish now. I was running out of ideas on how to get myself going again. Music was out the question, I didn't want to eat anything even though again, I knew I probably should. So, I just sat there, staring at the trees across the path, feeling like I might burst into tears.

A couple of runners went past, both asking if I was OK. I nodded and gave them a thumbs up, not really wanting to talk.

Another passed, again checking I was good.

"I'm just having a pity party; I'll be good in a minute," I replied, half smiling. At least some part of me knew I was being a total dick.

Saying it out loud had got me thinking. I took my phone out of my vest, praying that it would just work without me having to fight the touchscreen, and thankfully it did. I turned aeroplane mode off and waiting for the network indication to appear. It took a while, a horrible feeling growing that being on the seaward side of some big hills, there was unlikely to be any signal.

But my phone managed to reach out and grab the little bit of 4G drifting by, and I called the one person I knew would make me feel better.

I spent a few minutes chatting to Eva. She very nicely told me to get going, and get it done, there was no way I could quit now. I knew it, she knew it, and she knew I knew it too. It was lovely just to hear her voice.

She told me she'd been chatting with Oz, our youngest, and he'd been inspired enough by what I was up to that he thought entering one of those charity walking events as a family was a good idea. Blimey… he wasn't a big fan of walking, that was quite something! I *had* to finish now; I couldn't ruin that bit of inspiration.

As I was on the phone, a few more people went past, and every single one checked that I was OK. I love this sport (you wouldn't think so from all the bloody whinging I've been doing recently!), especially in the latter stages (are you *sure?!*). Everyone looks out for each other, and we all just want everyone else to do well and get to the end.

I finished the phone call, and just before putting my phone away I checked my messages. There was one from my daughter:

Hope your run is going well. KEEP GOINGGGGGGGG!!!!!!!!! Love you 💗🏃🏃👉

Involuntarily, my face formed a smile. I was smiling!

Phone back in aeroplane mode, into my vest. Six minutes had passed since I sat down on that log. Six minutes that had turned me around.

I didn't leap up, but I did try to get up purposefully. I'd accidentally inspired Eva and Oz into doing a walk event, and I imagined Soph sitting at university with her mates, dot watching with a bottle of vodka and much shouting going on, cheering me on. This wasn't about me any more – I couldn't let other people down. I had to get this done.

I started walking. Then I got faster. Then I got angry, and told the path that it wasn't going to stop me. Then I got angrier, and told some trees to fuck off. Then I told some ferns to fuck off as well. Then I told pretty much everything to fuck off, and keep fucking off until I was done! At which point I realised I was actually *running* - albeit slowly and very inelegantly, but running, nevertheless.

A moment later, at just before midday, I ran right across the totally unmarked border between Devon and Somerset.

Ahead was a sign:

Culbone: 3½ miles

I certainly hadn't covered a mile since the last sign, but much preferred the look of this one!

I wasn't back on top of the world, not totally overjoyed at getting on with the last bit of this race, but I definitely was out of the swamp of self-pity I'd been in ten minutes before.

All I had to do was get *out* of Porlock Weir – once I left the last checkpoint, there was absolutely no going back. I would have no choice but to carry on until the end, whatever state my head got into.

I judged that meant I had to stay positive for about another hour, then I could go into whatever embarrassingly pitiful state of despair I liked. I could have a sleep on the moors for all I cared, just get to Porlock, and get out of Porlock. An hour isn't so long…

The burst of energy that had inadvertently led to me doing some poor imitation of running had passed, and I was back to a plodding walk, but as I slowed, I kept telling myself to move faster, to push on, to get this done. I came up with a mantra that I kept repeating to myself: *The more I run, the quicker I'm done.*

The elation of the mood change gone; the ground was pissing me off again. The rocks were poking into my feet, my shoes clearly not cushioned enough for a comfortable ride along this sort of terrain. The woods were gloomy, and it felt like I'd been in them for hours, which, I suppose I had – about 2 hours anyway. I wasn't picking my feet up enough, and I was getting quite swearing by the third time I almost tripped over something. I really hope no-one was around to hear me turn the air blue!

The ground was constantly undulating, never a moment of flat. Some sections were technical – climbing on some roots around the base of a tree, or carefully stepping down steep slippery sections, that sort of thing.

The more I run, the quicker I'm done.

The path turned into more of a road, a sharp U-turn at the bottom of the hill where an old Land Rover came into view, parked outside a building – civilisation! At least to some degree.

As I walked down the hill towards the turn, over the wall to my left trees covered the side of the little valley, mostly hiding my view of a church. Being the smallest church in England, it wasn't difficult to hide St Bueno's. But I knew it was there, and I knew that meant it wasn't far to the checkpoint – less than 2 miles according to my watch.

Just get to Porlock and get out again. That was all I needed to do.

I knew somewhere around here was Ashley Combe, the summer retreat of Lady Ada Lovelace. The name may not mean much to many people, but Lovelace's fascination with mathematics allowed her to recognise that Babbage's Analytical Engine could do more than just pure calculations, her notes on the subject making her what is generally considered to be the first ever computer programmer. I've been banging away at computers for more than 40 years now, so it's somewhere that had some meaning to me, although I've never actually used the *Ada* programming language which is named after her.

I remembered the area having narrow paths edged with brick walls and unusual tunnels, all under heavy green tree cover, but I couldn't for the life of me remember where the hell the place was! Was it this side of Porlock Weir, or the far side? I was pretty sure there wasn't much in the way of wooded areas on the other side of the checkpoint, logic dictating that it was most likely something I should be coming up to soon. On this twisting path in the woods, you couldn't see very far ahead at all, so it might be just around the corner.

Situations like this are good – they keep the brain occupied, trying to drum up a solution to an unanswerable question, rather than thinking about how sore my back was or how tired my legs were.

The more I run, the quicker I'm done.

A turn on the path revealed a dark hole in the bricks ahead, answering the question of where Ashley Combe was. Ada Lovelace's husband, Lord William King, was an engineer and had a fascination with tunnels. While developing the estate, he created a special path with various tunnels through which tradesmen brought their carts to do work, so as not to be seen by the occupants of the house. I ducked my head to go through one of the few remaining examples, more out of instinct than necessity as the roof was actually quite high. It was dark inside, the air damp, the ground leaf covered, but only for a few seconds, then I was back out into the tree-muted daylight.

A little further ahead, through another smaller tunnel, I came to Worthy Toll Gate, a curved stone structure with two archways, some tiny windows towards the top and a nice-looking thatched roof. The coast path route headed a little way down Worthy Toll Road before turning back onto a path under some trees.

The trees became less dense, and the sky appeared first in patches, then in all its blue glory. The trail opened out, and there were people – normal people, not weirdo's running stupid distances! I was almost shaking with excitement and anticipation at getting to the checkpoint.

The path went around the edge of a grassy patch, then came to a gate that I went through and down a little path with houses either side which had me thinking I'd gone the wrong way… although the coast path acorn sign on the gate had been very clear. Under an arch, then I came out onto a road through a gap between two buildings, one of which was the Ship Inn, Porlock Weir.

The pub garden was busy with people, some of whom were looking over at the staggering idiot who'd just appeared, stopped, and then looked confused next to the pub.

I was looking around for a Climb South West flag, or some sign of where the checkpoint was. Nothing. And no-one around looked like they had the vaguest idea of what the hell I was up to.

Except one person. A woman was sat on the ground by the entrance to the car park opposite, looking over in my direction and smiling.

"You need to go round there," she said, pointing towards the back of the card park.

"Thanks!" I said, relieved, as I passed her on my way into the car park, heading in the way she'd been pointing.

Still nothing, just a car park. I kept going, and at the far side, on a triangular patch of grass between the car park and the road, was a big flag, a couple of tables, some deck chairs, and a few very knackered looking people.

Checkpoint 6 – Porlock Weir	
Distance	**103 miles**
Elevation	**17,075ft**
Time	**13:38 – 13:51** (target: 14:31, cut-off: 17:00)
Elapsed Time	**29 hours 42 minutes**
Position	**9th**
Split Position	**10th**

110 Mile Competitors Remaining: 15

I was so, so glad to see the back of that section. Lymouth to Porlock Wier had been absolutely horrible. Entirely down to my brain, of course. On a normal day, a walk in the woods along there would be amazing. There were so many things to see – amazing vegetation, interesting routes (and roots!), tiny churches, fountains, old houses, tunnels and more. But when you're trying to get through it as quickly as possible, to get on towards the end of your race, it feels like the place is designed to slow you down and keep you trapped in its gloomy interior.

At the checkpoint, the people running it were doing everything they could to look after the few of us that were there, all of us looking somewhat worse for wear. As I arrived, another chap was just leaving so I was instructed to plonk myself down in the garden chair on the grass. I unclipped my vest and carefully took it off my back, wincing as I peeled it away from my top. I didn't want to think about what state my back was in, I'd deal with that at the end of the event.

My soft flasks were whisked away, and a cup of coffee appeared in my hand, as if by magic. Then I was offered a piece of cake.

"I'm not sure I can stomach it to be honest," I started.

"It's home-made, it'll do you good," came the reply. "It's ginger cake."

Ginger cake... I do love ginger cake!

"Oh, go on then!"

A great wodge of cake was handed over on a paper plate, and boy, did it go down well!

Whilst munching on the cake, I dialled in the next – and final – section into my watch and took a look at the elevation profile.

I knew there was a big hill coming up which I thought was pretty close to Porlock, but the elevation profile had a long flat section at the start which I guessed to be about 3 miles. Very nice! Rather than getting straight into the hill, I'd get 3 miles of easy-going terrain, leaving just about 6 miles to go to the end… or only about 5 miles to go once I was at the top of the hill.

Five miles. Not much. Less than 2 parkruns. Not even a 10K race. Less than pretty much every training run I've done in the last year. And it looked generally flat or downhill. A veritable walk in the park.

The only slight dampener was the way Bossington Hill looked on the profile. It was steep, and it was very tall, a big lump on the watch screen. There was no doubt about it, that hill was definitely going to be hard work!

I was chatting to Liza French who was crewing at the checkpoint, and out of the blue, she happened to mention that she did the 110-mile race last year and that at this point her back was rubbed raw from her pack. A guy working at this aid station had rubbed a load of Sudocrem in which really helped.

"Well, that's one hell of a coincidence," I started, "because for the first time ever in an ultra, my pack has completely shredded my back and it's bloody painful!"

Now, when you volunteer to crew at an aid station, you expect to be met with tired and potentially injured runners, you might have to do a bit of cleaning up a minor wound and sticking on a plaster, massaging a leg, dealing with grumpy people, that sort of thing. I think it's a little above-and-beyond the call of duty rub a load of Sudocrem into a manky, sweaty, shredded back.

But that's exactly what Liza did for me, and I was so grateful!

It stung a bit as she rubbed a literal bucketload of the stuff into my back, with a warning that it'll probably never completely come out of the top I was wearing. I could not have cared less.

I thanked her again and again, it really was a wonderfully kind thing to do and within moments after getting my top back on, it was starting to feel better. Not perfect, there was still some pain, but it was somehow more manageable. I'm not sure how much of it was placebo effect, but it didn't matter. The thing I needed to do my best to control wasn't the physical pain, but the mental attitude, and anything that felt positive – like a reduction in back pain – would be helping.

With the ginger cake long gone, and the last of my coffee finished, I swung my race vest back onto my shoulders, pleasantly surprised – no, *delighted* – by the lack of pain compared to just a few minutes before. Poles in hand, I double checked the direction and shouted a few more thank-you's to the frankly wonderful crew.

Fed, watered, and back smothered in sticky white Sudocrem, I headed off with an inner glow – the knowledge that I'd just left the final checkpoint on the North Coast 110 race.

25

"True freedom doesn't lie in the maximization of choice, but, ironically, is most easily found in a life where there is little choice."

- *Steve Hagan, Buddhism Plain and Simple*

Saturday, 13:51

The first step away from Porlock Weir checkpoint was the beginning of the end. I'd done it. I'd essentially finished the North Coast 110-mile race. I hadn't quit! It was now just one foot in front of the other until the end. All choice had been removed – there was nowhere else to call it a day other than the end, and it was now just simple, easy, mentally untaxing.

I mean... well... I still obviously had a few more steps to go. Maybe, er... 3 or 4 hours. Oh bugger. That sounds like a long way now.

The route ahead was along the road at the back of a pebbly beach. In the distance, the lump of Bossington Hill sat ominously, although looking deceptively manageable from this distance.

With the going simple for a bit, I got my phone out and called Eva to let her know that I'd grown some bollocks, zipped up my man-suit, got out of the rut and all the other metaphors that I could think of... I was on my way to the finish. She sounded quite relieved (she knows how absolutely intolerable I'd be had I got home having not finished!), and while chatting away I almost missed a turn off the nice tarmac road, down some steps and onto the pebbles of the beach.

I didn't much like the look of this bit – pebbles are a pain to walk on – so I finished the call, put my phone away and readied myself for a trudge along the stones.

I was right. They were annoying – slippery, hard work on my ankles and continuously prodding through those too-thin shoes. And they slowed me down when I just wanted to be making good progress.

Some way in front, a couple of walkers kept stopping to inspect the stones, occasionally picking one or two up and pocketing them. I'm not quite sure what they were up to, but it was handy having them ahead as they showed me the way to go along the ridge of pebbles that connected us. I mean, at this point, I was assuming they were going the same way as me, and it seemed to match up with the route on the watch.

It wasn't immediately obvious where the path continued after the beach, the pebbles stretched on forever, but the line on my wrist showed a hard right turn coming up. I hobbled my way along the stones some more, then turned and headed up the bank away from the sea at the point where my watch was suggested I should turn off the beach. There didn't appear to be anything there – no obvious path, marker or anything to indicate I was going the right way, and the pebble bank ahead shielded my view from anything beyond.

As I approached the top, I caught sight of a little bright orange Climb South West sign with a black arrow marking the direction and breathed a silent sigh of relief that I was definitely going in the right direction.

The climb on the pebbles wasn't high, but it was annoying, with me slipping down a couple of times due to my tiredness and general ineptitude. Cresting the summit, if you could call it that, I was met with a flat plain stretching out ahead, an obvious path cutting its way along the ground. The pebbles of the beach faded out, being replaced with soft short grass underfoot, a welcome relief.

The path headed inland on a decent bit of soft, level ground. To the left, Porlock Marsh stretched across towards Bossington. At the end of 1996, severe storms caused the sea to flood over the shingle barrier beach and flood the marshland, forever changing the ecosystem. The change provided the perfect environment for rare coastal plants and wildlife, and the area has been designated a Site of Special Scientific Interest since 2002.

I headed alongside the western edge of the marsh away from the beach and towards the town of Porlock (as opposed to Porlock Weir which I'd just come from). A 90-degree left turn at the back of the marsh had me heading towards a barn in the distance. Alongside me as I walked was the famous row of stunted, dead trees, killed when the ground was flooded with saltwater, leaving the bare branches reaching up to the sky like an army of wooden monsters.

In the distance, a guy who had the look of someone in the race was walking along purposefully. I passed an elderly couple walking in the other direction, we exchange a brief greeting, and for once I was happy to just carry on and not have a conversation about the race that was going on around them.

I passed the barn and was looking out for the memorial to the Bossington plane crash of 29th October 1942. A US Air Force Liberator plane was returning from a U-boat patrol mission over the Bay of Biscay when, due to heavy rain and poor visibility, it clipped the top of Bossington Hill, crashing into Porlock Marsh and killing 11 of the 12 on board. As I passed the monument, enclosed behind a small wooden fence, I tapped my head in a little salute, a small attempt to show respect for the lives of the airmen.

I eventually caught up with the guy I'd spotted ahead and we carried on together, having a decent chat as we both went along the flat route to Bossington village.

His name was Chris (there are a lot of Chris's, aren't there?), and he was having a problem with his ITB (iliotibial band – the fascia that runs from your hip down to your knee on the outside of your leg and can often cause troubling knee pain during the repetitive movements of long running events). Because of this, he couldn't run any more, but could walk OK. Exactly the same thing happened to me about half way into the 145-mile Kennet and Avon Canal Race a few years before – every time I tried running, my knee locked up, but I could comfortably walk fast without issue. He was finding that he didn't like going down hills, but didn't have a problem with climbing – handy, considering what was coming in the next mile or two!

I found out too that Chris worked at a gym in London and had recently done a photoshoot for some body-building stuff, so I assume he knew how to lift a weight or two. Unlike most runners, he probably had some decent core and upper body strength, great attributes for holding yourself together on long adventures like this one, and something to improve in myself for that very reason.

He'd done some triathlons while in the Army and had finished the Weymouth Half Iron Man a few months before, but today, doing the 55km North Coast race, was the longest run he'd ever done.

All that chatting had made the distance to Bossington disappear in a blur of gates and tree-lined paths and soon we turned on to a tarmac road by a marker indicating that Porlock Weir was 3 miles behind us. That went quickly, only about 6 miles left to go now. Oh, and one bloody great hill.

As we reached a beautiful looking cottage on the left, Chris's partner was waiting on the other side of the road so we said goodbye and I carried on along the road, hoping the route would be obvious as I was currently heading away from the bulk of the hill that I thought I was supposed to be climbing soon.

It was all fine really, the road continued down past more lovely looking houses in this peaceful village, then round to the left and into the National Trust car park.

On the far side, in the trees, was a footbridge over the River Horner and what looked a lot like a coast path marker, so I headed over in that direction, keeping an eye on my watch for confirmation.

People had parked up in the car park and were out and about enjoying the sunny but not overly hot Saturday afternoon. Kids and dogs were splashing about in the water, and people were walking slowly along the riverside path.

Along I came, clacking away with my poles, storming past everyone having somehow found a small burst of energy to get the pace up a bit. I was apprehensive about the mountain I was about to climb, I just wanted to get on with it now, so was trying to go as quickly as I could along the flat sections.

The path left the river and headed a little to the right but stayed almost level for far longer than I expected as I skirted around the base of Bossington Hill. But then the inevitable happened, and the path started to rise up.

Initially, it wasn't much of a climb, and I tried to attack it with some enthusiasm and effort. But you can have all the enthusiasm you like (and I didn't really have that much to be honest), but if your energy levels are shot to pieces then it very quickly becomes apparent you ain't gonna be storming up the hill today.

A minute or so after starting to climb, the path took a sharp right turn and began heading properly up the side of the hill, the true extent of the climb now clearly visible ahead. Amazingly, I'd manage to pass a couple of people, and as I reached a gate, I held it open for them, taking a moment to relax, breathe and ready myself for what I was about to do.

Chris caught back up with me a little after the gate, and was moving well, his ITB problem giving him no issue on the climb. We said a quick hello and goodbye as he powered on ahead and disappeared into the distance up the hill.

I got my head into determined climbing mode, slow but continuous progress. One foot in front of the other.

I knew the hill was just about 1,000ft tall, and the maps I had on my watch showed contour lines. A little further ahead on my screen was one marked, rather arbitrarily, at 417ft. I judged my height right now to be around 100ft, so it wouldn't be long to get to that higher contour and then I'd have about half the hill ticked off, at least if you round up quite considerably.

My feet kept pushing against the ground, my legs kept lifting me a little higher, and I kept looking at my watch. According to that rather wonderful modern technology, I seemed to be standing still.

I kept going, turning my feet to the sides to make the climb feel a little easier as I went, leaning heavily on my poles. I wasn't out of breath, I didn't have the energy to raise my effort level to the point where I was aerobically challenged. I was just hardly moving.

I climbed for 5 minutes. I was at 200ft. I climbed for 5 more minutes; I was at 300ft.

OK, it probably wasn't quite as long as that, but my progress felt absolutely glacial.

I looked up the hill as I climbed, trying to pick features like bushes or cracks in the ground to target and tick off, to break the climb down to something more manageable than the whole thing.

A paraglider circled around above my head, silently taunting me.

600ft.

700ft.

800ft.

Eventually, after what felt like an eternity, the hill started to level off. It had taken me almost exactly 30 minutes to cover 1 single mile.

I wasn't at the top yet, but the terrain was beginning to get much flatter, although I lacked the energy to capitalise on this with any sort of pace. That hill had really stripped away the last of my reserves of energy – physically, I was spent.

But, for a change on this particular day, I was mentally in a pretty good place. I'd just almost finished the final climb of the whole race. It was all downhill from here, both metaphorically and, I hoped, physically. I could pretty much lay on my side and roll to the end.

A group of walkers were sat on a bench at the top discussing some of the features you could see from this great height. They seemed aware of what the steady stream of generally exhausted people were up to too. They congratulated me on my ascent, and told me the top wasn't far away, just the lump visible a little way in the distance and not too much higher.

I stood for a moment taking in the view from this 1,000ft vantage point. And what a view it was. Green grass, spotted with patches of darker heather led away in front of me, then suddenly disappeared off the edge of the hill. At the bottom, the darker area of Porlock Marsh looked a million miles away, and the lumpy extent of the coast through north Devon was visible all the way back to Foreland Point just this side of Lynmouth.

I started off again continuing in the direction I'd been going up the hill, heading towards the summit, Selworthy Beacon.

Ahead was another racer who was walking along after that beast of a climb, but amazingly I actually seemed to be gaining on them. As I headed up the path towards the summit, I caught up with her and we did the usual mid-ultramarathon exchange.

"How are you doing?"

"I'm exhausted, how about you?"

"Yeah, absolutely knackered. But not far to go now."

The problem with heading towards Selworthy Beacon was that we weren't supposed to go to Selworthy Beacon. I noticed this as I glanced at my watch shortly after we had both totally ignored a turn and just carried on straight.

"We're supposed to be over there," I said, pointing to our left.

"Are you sure?" She didn't sound convinced.

"Yep." So much so that I immediately turned in that direction and started tramping across a load of heather to find an unseen path. Thirty seconds later, as the heather got higher and a load of gorse appeared, making the detour somewhat less pleasant, I was beginning to be slightly less sure of my navigational ability, what with my history in that particular area of expertise. Thankfully, I spotted a wide track ahead, pushed through a final particularly big chunk of gorse and popped out onto the right route.

The woman I was with seemed far from impressed by my detour, and shortly after we got out onto the track, she found the energy to start running. I had none of that left in me, so I watched her run off into the distance.

Back on my own again, which, to be honest, I was more than happy with. I like catching up with people as it presents a challenge, but this late in a race, when I'm so tired, trying to conjure up some scintillating conversation is difficult. It's needs to be a two-way thing, and if there's no immediate connection when chatting, there's no point in sticking together.

On I went, alone, exhausted, but getting more excited with each step. I was almost there!

26

A haze of glory

Saturday, 15:25

Big Bastard Bossington Hill had been summitted, and now I had less than 5 miles to go. That's hardly anything! Forty-five minutes on a gentle run round the block, obviously a bit longer with these stupid broken legs, but still, it was all downhill now on nice gentle moorland, it'll be quick and easy.

The first thing that annoyed me (or about the millionth thing, if you're counting from the start of the race rather than the last 10 seconds) was that I'd thought the route was all on flat, grassy ground. Nice gentle moorland, soft and cushioned. That's how I'd remembered it from the walk last year.

But I'd remembered wrong, not for the first time. The path was on a track. A stony track, with potholes and jutting rocks, a few slippery pebbles and bits of general moorland debris that I had to work to avoid.

It was playing havoc with my feet. No more than any other section, it's just that when your feet have been battered from the bottom by rocks and stones and roots for mile upon mile of trails, it's really bloody annoying when you get even more at a point where you were hoping for flat, spongy grass.

The speed that I was going was another factor. Five miles doesn't take 45 minutes when you're taking 20 minutes to cover a mile. It takes the best part of 2 hours. And I didn't want to be out here for another 2 hours.

I was working to pick up the pace, trying to push along and get some of that fast-walking magic involved in my movement. I kept checking my watch, and the best I could manage was hints of 17-minute-something per mile at my fastest.

There are loads of navigation metrics on my watch, and I turn most of them off because they're unnecessary. But I do find both the ETA (estimated time of arrival) and ETE (estimated time enroute) useful, especially at this point as you're trying to knock down those miles to the end of a race.

I wasn't looking at the ETA – what time I was going to arrive – I couldn't care less. What I was more interested in was the ETE, or how long I had left, and despite my attempts at putting in some effort it was still showing over 1 hour to go.

Not much, considering what I'd already done. But there's something psychologically "big" about an hour when you just want something over with. A couple of minutes you can lose in a daydream, but an hour… you're going to feel pretty much every part of that hour as it goes past.

I had a think about the numbers, and they didn't seem to quite add up. I realised that the average pace the watch was using would be taking into account my climb up Bossington Hill. OK, I wasn't moving fast right now, but I was going a damn sight faster than when I was going up that hill, so my watch was giving me times that were heavily biased towards the slow side.

I fired up my brainbox computer and did a quick calculation. A mere 10 minutes later, I'd multiplied a couple of numbers together, and worked out that it would be 58 minutes! Sadly, like in the Hitchhikers Guide to the Galaxy, I had absolutely no idea what the question was any more. Still, it turns out that by trying to do some basic maths in your head after being awake for over 30 hours and having covered a good chunk over 100 miles on foot in that time, you can actually pass quite a bit of time!

For once, my watch was right in its display of the elevation profile – the route really was mostly flat or gently downhill. Being a simple track across moorland, there wasn't much to watch out for, I just had to keep following the line on my wrist and watch the numbers go down.

I was caught and overtaken by 2 separate people, one doing the 110km race, and the other the 55km one. We had brief exchanges as we passed, but it added an element of excitement spotting them in the distance behind me, waiting a couple of minutes for them to catch up and then watching them disappear into the distance for a few more minutes. That passed another 5 minutes as I plodded on in something of a dream state, half way between awake and asleep.

With so little to go now the finish was inevitable, and although I was genuinely exhausted, I was feeling really positive. Rather than focusing on the negatives of my current situation like I had been a few hours before, I was picking out little things that were actually boosting me. Like my back. That Sudocrem had worked wonders, and although I could still tell the skin was in a bit of a mess, it really wasn't seriously bothering me anymore. That was maybe also because I was moving so slowly, but again, thinking positively, I was holding on to that 17-ish minute mile pace and not slowing down significantly.

The simplicity of the route had meant that at the top of Bossington Hill, my watch had indicated that the next significant turn was 3.4 miles away. That distance had been gradually dropping and now had almost completely passed – I was in sight of a gate and a marker post indicating a turn to the left, just as a guy doing the 55k race caught up with me.

His ITB had also started giving him some grief, seemingly a common theme among the 55k race people! So, with that, he walked along with me a for a bit. As we passed through the gate, my watch beeped to indicate that we'd gone through the turn and gave me a distance of 2.4 miles, with a little finish flag next to the numbers. Just over 3,800 metres to go and it would all be over. So close!

Mr 55k and I got on well, a palpable sense of excitement in the air at being so close to the end. We were moving along the now gently descending trail into some woods and having a nice chat. I was waffling on about all sorts of nonsense, and I remember becoming slightly aware that I was probably talking too much, but I was too tired to make sense of it all. You know when you've had a few drinks and you think you're really interesting and clever, but in fact you're slurring and boring as hell? It was probably like that, and I offer my apologies to Mr 55k for my rambling incoherence!

The path started followed a long zig-zag route down the side of the hill into Minehead. The turn we'd made at the top was a little over 750ft above sea level, so we had quite a way to drop down, and a switch back trail made it about as nice as it could be in terms of steepness. The route was in woods though, and it brought back flashbacks of the wooded section between Lynmouth and Porlock Weir – colourful leaves on the ground hiding hazardous stones and roots, and plenty of pointy things to stick into my feet. The downhill gradient was bringing back the pack-bouncing with each step too, which was most unappreciated.

Not long later – a few minutes at most – the wooded section ended, the roots disappearing leaving just a smooth track under the trees, descending down the final section to the coast path route that ran flat along to Minehead seafront and the South West Coast Path marker.

In my head, once I got to the bottom of this zig-zag section and down to pretty much sea level – which felt imminent – I was done, that was the end of having to put in effort. I'm not sure if I thought I was just going to magically float to the end or something, but the spell was broken with some dismay when I checked my watch and found that I had 1¼ miles left to the end!

It doesn't sound much, but at the pace I was going, it would be 25 minutes or so. Imagine thinking you're 2 or 3 minutes from sanctuary, and someone then adds 20 minutes to it!

But, again, my unusually, amazingly cheerful brain kicked in – 20 minutes isn't long. Think about what you've already done, it said. You're almost there. Get on with it and stop bloody moaning!

Mr 55k thanked me for the conversation on the way down the hill and said he was going to pick up pace a bit. I wished him well on his quest to get to the end, and he started off at a slow run, something I could only dream of now.

I was sniffing distance from the end, but it was still a little out of reach. I kept descending in the trees, those never-ending trees, hoping I would hit the flat promenade and the end would be right there in front of me…

I put one foot in front of the other, then repeated, and kept going. Soon, the trees came to an end. I was in a flat green grassy space with a path through the middle. A couple with a young child looked behind to see what the clacking sound was, saw me coming along and eased themselves off the path onto the grass. I'm not sure if they were being polite or were a little nervous of the strange bloke staggering along towards them, but I appreciated it either way as it made my passage easier. A straight line along a path is easier than curving onto the grass. Not by much, but little amounts matter after 109-and-a-bit miles!

A little further along another couple saw me powering my way along, looking like a zombie on a mission, and they also stepped from the path onto the grass to let me pass. The woman caught sight of my number and exclaimed "110 miles!?".

"Yeah," I replied, with a slightly deranged grin.

"When did you start?"

"About 8 yesterday morning from Hartland Quay"

"Oh my god!", and that open mouthed look. That one – that one right there – I'd earnt that! I wasn't *going* to do 110 miles; I'd just *done* 110 miles! I grinned back, aiming for happy but probably looking like a mentally challenged Cheshire cat, and carried on power-walking the last few minutes of my race.

The path came to the roundabout at the end of Quay West, the road I'd been waiting on for a minibus about 36 hours earlier. As I reached the road, I was met by Lyds (Lydia), one of the Climb South West crew. She was bright and bubbly, just the sort of person you want at this point, all smiles and congratulations. It was infectious, and I just couldn't stop grinning!

I'd never met Lyds before, but it turns out she lives in the same area as I do and recognised me from running around the mean streets of Dorset. It's a small world, even smaller when you start mixing with people insane enough to think running 100-plus miles is a good idea!

She walked down the road with me, chatting away, her excited beaming smile making me feel really special, really proud to have got to this point. We went along the final bit of road, her guiding me along a section with no pavement outside the Old Ship Aground hotel, making sure I didn't get spread over the road by an oncoming car.

And there it was.

Just ahead, I could see the South West Coast Path marker, the one I'd been next to a day-and-a-half ago. A sight I really hadn't been entirely confidence in seeing again today.

But there it was, in front of me.

The end of the race!

Lyds said goodbye and went back to support other finishers as they came to the end of their race, while I carried on the last few metres towards Justin and the Climb South West crew at the finish line by the marker.

They were clapping and cheering, and I felt I needed to put on a bit of a show, so I ran… I say ran; I mean staggered, obviously. But it got more of a cheer, and I was grinning from ear to ear!

As I got to them, I stopped my watch, but they were cheerfully shouting to me about something. It took me a second to process the noise and realise they were telling me I had to touch the coast path marker to finish. I turned and took the few steps to the great big metal map, spread open, with the route that I'd just done a part of the overall track shown on the south west peninsula of England. I put my hands out and rested against the marker, closed my eyes, and soaked up the moment. I'd done it!

As I returned back to Justin, he warned me to stop before crossing the line on the ground marking the start of the West Somerset Coast Path, otherwise I'd have to do that as well! Er… no fucking way, mate!

At just past a quarter to five on Saturday, 8th October, I completed the North Coast 110-mile race in an official time of 32 hours 49 minutes and 15 seconds.

Finish – SWCP marker, Minehead	
Distance	**112 miles**
Elevation	**18,200ft**
Time	**16:45:15** (target: 18:06, cut-off: 21:30)
Elapsed Time	**32 hours 49 minutes 15 seconds**
Position	**9**[th]
Split Position	**11**[th]
	110 Mile Finishers: **15**

Overall win taken by Matthew Hart in 23:21:22
First female was Emma Brock: 29:53:45 (4th place overall)

Justin fished around in his jacket pockets, trying to remember which side had the 110-mile buckle in, then he produced the gleaming silver lump of metal – the reward for just under 33 hours of slog!

There was something refreshing and pure about the low-key nature of the end. I do love events like the Arc of Attrition, but it's become a big spectacle, something which I think a lot of people really love. I'm in two minds – it's great to have a busy finish and lots of help on the course, but sometimes it's really refreshing just to finish a long race, get a pat on the back and be sent on your way.

Armed with my hard-earned buckle, Justin took a couple of photos with his phone of me standing against the South West Coast Path marker, holding up the buckle and still grinning like an idiot. I was bathing in the joy of not having to move anymore!

I'd completed it. It certainly wasn't a given, and there were times when the dream of reaching this finish line seemed like a fading dream, slipping away from my reach. But I'd got to the end. I didn't have the disappointment or the need to attempt some sort of justification for a DNF (Did Not Finish) to contend with, just the glow of a successful race.

I kept thinking about Type 2 fun: the concept of getting the sense of fun through the achievement of doing something that, at the time, you essentially hate. I tried to hold on to how I felt right now, at the end, so I could compare it to how I felt a day later.

Even 24 hours, with a bit of sleep and recovery, can completely change your memory of the events. Not the details of what happened so much, but the nuances of how you *felt*. Twelve hours before I finished, I was smothered in a blanket of pure, unadulterated dismay, having been awake for so long and having so much left to do. I never, ever wanted to do another ultramarathon again, I distinctly remember that.

Now, standing just a minute or two over the finish line, I was beginning to think... maybe it wasn't all *that* bad...

I dug around on Garmin Connect after the race and here's a few statistics about my North Coast 110-mile race:

Distance	**112.2 miles**
Time	**32:49:15**
Pace	**17:03/mile average**
Ascent	**18,204ft**
Calories	**10,963 calories**
Steps	**217,539**

27

After the Finish

Bea was sat on the sea wall by the finish, a big smile on her face. I'm not one to do this often, especially with someone I've only just met, but I headed over and we hugged, congratulating each other. You build a tight bond with someone when you both push yourselves close to your limits.

She had done amazingly well, pushing on in that final section and building over an hour lead on my time, finishing in 31 hours 43 minutes in 7th place and 2nd lady.

Andy Mutter was at the finish too, and he'd kept moving well from Combe Martin, crossing the line in 32 hours 8 minutes, 8th place, and he was the last 110-mile finisher before me.

Matt Dalton, who I'd run along chatting with in the early stages of the race around Clovelly had covered the distance in 30 hours 26 minutes coming 5th, his 10th (at-least-)100-miler of the year, with two more planned before the end of December, all in aid of raising money for Prostate Cancer UK.

Andy Quicke – the guy who'd caught up with us in the bus the previous morning and left his car in Lynmouth – finished in 3rd place in a bloody quick(e) 26 hours 55 minutes – that race to catch the bus to the start was well worth it!

I'd spent a good chunk of time with Chris Roberts as well, coming into Westward Ho!, and then from a little after Barnstaple all the way through to Baggy Point, where his painful foot had slowed him down. Bea and I had gone on ahead there, and Chris had made his way to the next checkpoint at Woolacombe, but I guess his foot had got the better of him by then and his race ended there.

In a bid to reduce waste, there were no specific finisher t-shirts for the race this year, but there were some boxes in the shelter by the finish which held leftovers from the previous years. My attitude to unnecessary things has changed a lot over time, and I completely agree with not producing things that people don't want. On the other hand, I use running t-shirts until they literally fall apart, and this was quite a race to be able to quietly shout about through the graphics on your top! I dug out a nice black medium t-shirt with Hartland Point lighthouse adoring the front and "110" mentioned more than once.

I said my thank yous and goodbyes to the organisers and fellow competitors alike, and began heading back to my car. It took a moment to realise that what I was carrying felt significantly lighter than it had walking from the car the previous morning, and moments later I was back in the shelter picking up my drop bag. I think I can be forgiven for forgetting it considering what little sleep I'd had over the last 2 days!

I staggered my way back to the car. In all honesty, it was a surprisingly unstaggery stagger, walking almost like a very tired – but not broken – human being. Ten minutes after leaving the seafront finish, I was back at my car having covered about 100 metres... ok, maybe it was a bit more staggery than I thought.

For the final time, I took my race vest off my back, the burning pain dulled a little by the blessed relief of knowing that I wasn't going to be putting the bloody thing back on again!

I opened the back of my race vest, extracted one of the drybags and then dug around in its depths, eventually finding the small bag that contained my car key. It was a relief to find it still there! I dumped everything running related into the boot of the car, picked up the big red rucksack that I'd sensibly pre-loaded with everything I'd need for the night, and locked the car up. Despite my back, I didn't want to have to carry the rucksack in my hand, so I did swing it round over my shoulders. The padded back sat far more comfortably than my race vest and taking it very slowly I headed off on the walk back to the hotel.

Google Maps said 8 minutes. It took me 20. But it wasn't wholly unpleasant, my head still in the happy place of having just finished a 110-mile race and now heading towards food, drink and rest. My legs were happy they didn't have to work hard trying to get there as quickly as possible, but could instead just plod along at a slow walk, at whatever pace felt comfortable.

Back at the hotel, I checked in and was sent up to the same room. I'm not entirely sure what happened with the bill... when I went to pay, they said it was already paid, so I didn't argue!

Up in the room, I dumped my bag on the floor, went into the bathroom, and got a big towel which I spread on the bed to catch any manky leakages that might escape from my back, then lay down. The feeling was *exquisite*. Even though my back and legs hurt like hell, I was laying down, flat on my back, comfortable on the soft bed. I closed my eyes for a moment to soak up the feeling, then got my phone out and called Eva.

I was trying to put off having a shower for as long as possible, the thought of peeling my top away from my raw back really not something I was looking forward to. After a nice but somewhat incoherent chat with Eva (the incoherence entirely my fault), I thought I'd inflict the same thing on my sister. Ten minutes and two phone calls after laying down on the bed, I couldn't put it off any more.

In the end, the shower wasn't *too* bad. The top came off easily thanks, in part, to the smothering of Sudocrem that Liza had applied back at Porlock Weir.

After the shower, I held my phone out behind me and took a photo of my back as it was the only way I could see the state it was in. I immediately wished I hadn't. I've had sections of my lower back rubbed to the point of being quite red after ultras before, but this was different. The top few layers of skin were removed in big chunks on both my lower and middle back, shiny raw patches clearly visible. No wonder the bloody thing hurt!

I stuck on some slouchy jogging bottoms that I wouldn't normally be seen dead in outside the house but were probably considered smart-casual for Wetherspoons, donned my new NC110 t-shirt and headed down for some food.

There's only one thing you can order when you've just covered 110 miles on foot – the biggest thing on the menu! I tapped away on the Wetherspoons app, and soon a pint of Guinness was on the table and 2,000 calories of Empire State Burger, chips, and onion rings on their way.

When the food turned up, I'd had about 20% of the pint of Guinness and I felt as pissed as a fart. My eyes couldn't see straight and saw double the amount of onion rings I should have had. I then realised I'd accidentally ordered extra onion rings, and there were, in fact, 12 of them.

I'd been looking forward to this moment – guilt free food and drink while revelling in my epic achievement! But my imagination was bigger than my stomach and I struggled to eat, despite my massive lack of calories over the last day and a half. By the time the burger and Guinness was gone, I felt like I was either going to be sick or pass out from a combination of the alcohol and tiredness, so I left the rest, figuring it was time to go to bed despite it only being a little after 6pm.

Back in the room, I lay down on my back on the bed, the towel still in place as I was pretty sure I my back was going to make a mess. It was a little painful to lay down, but after a few minutes of laying still my back pain paled into insignificance compared to the deep ache right in the middle of my thighs, like the bones themselves were on fire. I had a couple of paracetamol and lay back down, half drunk, half dead from tiredness, but in so much overall aching discomfort that I did wonder if I'd actually get to sleep.

I woke around 10pm with my legs feeling a million times better, got into a more comfortable position, and fell back to sleep to the sound of that incredibly noisy extractor fan from the kitchen below.

It was restless all night, and around 5:30am I woke with a feeling that I wasn't going to get back to sleep, my body clock all over the place like I had jetlag. I had a wash, stuck on loose clothes and sat down at the desk with my iPad, writing down notes about everything I could remember from the race while it was still fresh in my head.

I held off until 8am for breakfast. Sat down in the pub with a large fried breakfast and several much-needed cups of strong black coffee, I carried on with the notes.

All fed and watered, there was nothing left to do now. Back in the room, I grimaced at the state of the towel, pillow and bedsheet, my leaky back having decorated it in a way which was definitely going to raise a few questions from the people cleaning the room – sorry! I didn't bother changing clothes – I didn't care what the people of Minehead thought of my slouchy trousers – and headed out with my pack on my back, which having scabbed over a little was feeling generally better, but with occasional sharp pains as I moved and split the surface in places.

The drive home was mostly uneventful, with just enough coffee in my system to keep me awake and out of trouble. Although the tiredness did have an unusual side effect – I had an uninvited guest in my mind, and no matter how much I tried, I couldn't get rid of it. In the voice of Clive Gollings, Nick Frost's character in the movie Paul, the single phrase kept going around in my head:

"That was good, wasn't it?"[14]

---

[14] If you haven't seen Paul (from 2011) and like Simon Pegg & Nick Frost films like Shaun of the Dead, Hot Fuzz etc, then you should watch it! The voice in my head was saying it in exactly the way Nick Frost does near the end of the film, you'll understand why when you see it!

Epilogue

Striving for better

The end of 2022 wasn't a great time for me. After the North Coast 110, I allowed myself a physical and mental time-out under the guise of "recovery", but I was just using it as an excuse.

As has been the recurring theme, I ate badly and got back to drinking way too much, but this time I had no event on the horizon, no new adventure to look forward to and, more importantly, be fit and healthy for.

My running dropped right down again. Looking back over the year, this had been a pattern after each ultra I'd run, but the first 3 were close enough together that it almost went unnoticed. After June – when I entered the North Coast race – I picked right up, lots of miles, lots of hours each month. But the last 2 months of the year, I was running monthly mileages that I hadn't been down to in almost a decade – just over 30 miles during the whole of December.

Things went from bad to worse, a perfect storm of situations dragging me downwards mentally. A lack of target meant I had no motivation to stay fit, which gave fuel to my unhealthy lifestyle. Work stayed intense, and I used the free time from not running to do more, stay later, work harder, not always to great benefit. The end of the year brought darker mornings and evenings, and I locked myself away in an artificially illuminated office for most of the day.

Financial and family stresses brought things to a head in early December, and, without going into any details, I hit a mental low that I've never experienced before, and don't ever want to again.

It seems ridiculously self-centred to think that a target for my running – or rather, lack of one – could have such an effect on me. The other factors I mentioned above did exacerbate the situation, but I had a deep yearning for something that wasn't related to work, financial stress or anything like that – just pure escapism. An adventure.

Do you ever wonder what would happen if you stopped running? What sort of person you'd be?

I always thought I'd be fat, drunk and happy. I like eating, I like drinking, I usually don't like running much – at least not the "run around the block" sort of training runs. So, I just assumed that one day, I'd gracefully stop running, put on a few stone and get on with more important things like work, going to the tip, and DIY.

But I think I've realised that, at least now in my life, running is an important – dare I say *critical* – part of what I need. It somehow keeps me slightly to the saner side of completely bonkers.

After that low point in December, I stopped drinking. I was planning to do it for New Year anyway, but as I write this, I haven't touched any alcohol for 6 weeks – not much time in the scheme of things, but more importantly, I've no desire to go back to it.

For a lot of people, it's a fun, social lubricant, and they're perfectly able to drink sensible amounts, have a laugh and it not be a problem at all. I wouldn't class myself as an alcoholic, but I'm not one of those people that can just have one or two. Any excuse, and I'd have a drink. Not a bottle of vodka (usually), but a few beers. And when you're drinking a few beers pretty much every night – even when you're at home on your own – it's really not all that healthy for your body or your mind.

I spent a good amount of time over the Christmas break having a think about why I'd got so low and how to fix it.

One of the things I've realised about running is that while I meant what I said above – about not really liking running most of the time – it's not *quite* the right sentiment. No-one loves every dark, rainy run around your local streets that you've done a million times before, but there is something there... even when I've had real trouble getting out the door, am not really enjoying the run and want to get home, there's still a bit of me deep down inside that's relishing the feeling. The energy, the movement, the breathing, the experience, the freedom.

There always seems to be something else I *should* be doing instead of going for a run – work, going to the tip, DIY – which makes me feel a little like running isn't important, and I shouldn't be prioritising it, and that brings an obvious set of problems as to how I look at running.

But now I see both running and walking as something I need to do, something important to me, at least at this point in life. I still need to see if I've figured out how to stay motivated without something to train for, but it feels like, now, running isn't just preparation for some arbitrary target. It's a physical and mental requirement for me, a lifeline. Like a vitamin – essential, but it takes a fair amount of time not having it before you notice the negative effects. So, for now at least, I need to make sure I'm getting the right dose of Vitamin R.

Having said all that, I have very recently started making plans for a new adventure sometime in the next few months. I won't say too much yet, other than it won't cost much, involves a backpack and tent and I'm planning on writing a book about it (oh no, not another one!). Oh, and, amazingly for me, it's NOT on the South West Coast Path!

Hopefully next time we meet in the pages of a book, I won't be banging on about how I've gone off the rails, eaten too much, drank too much and generally been a bit of a plonker – that's surely getting a bit boring for everyone!

Until next time…

THE END

Before you go…

I genuinely hope you've enjoyed this book. If you did and have a few minutes to spare, I would be so grateful if you could leave a review (hopefully positive!) on Amazon, and maybe rave about how amazing it was to spend a few hours getting lost in these pages to all your friends on social media!

You can stay in at:

www.swcpplod.co.uk

and if you've got any questions or feedback, you can use the contact form or social media links on the site.

Thanks again for taking the time to read my book!

Printed in Great Britain
by Amazon